THE PASTORAL
PLAN

Studies in the Pastoral Epistles

Jeff Amsbaugh

Copyright © 2020 Jeff Amsbaugh. All rights reserved.

Writings contained herein are by the author unless otherwise stated.

No part of this publication may be reproduced, stored in a retrieval system or transmitted in any way by any means — electronic, mechanical, photocopy, recording or otherwise — without the prior permission of the copyright holder, except as provided by USA copyright law.

All Scriptures are taken from the King James Bible.

ISBN# 978-1-61119-231-5

Printed in the United States of America.
Printed by Calvary Publishing
A Ministry of Parker Memorial Baptist Church
1902 East Cavanaugh Road
Lansing, Michigan 48910
www.CalvaryPublishing.org

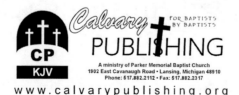

THE PASTORAL
P L A N

Studies in the Pastoral Epistles

Jeff Amsbaugh

TABLE OF CONTENTS

Chapter 1 - The Secure Message of the Pastor . 7

Chapter 2 - The Real Gospel 15

Chapter 3 - How the Gospel Fortifies the Pastor . 25

Chapter 4 - The Importance of Public Prayer. . 31

Chapter 5 - The Role of Women in Public Worship . 41

Chapter 6 - The Office of the Bishop . . . 49

Chapter 7 - The Duties of a Deacon . . . 57

Chapter 8 - The Reason for Order . . . 65

Chapter 9 - Errors That Plague the Church . . 73

Chapter 10 - Methods of Dealing with False Teachers 79

Chapter 11 - Dealing with Widows . . . 87

Chapter 12 - Honoring Your Pastors . . . 95

Chapter 13 - Slaves and Masters . . . 103

Chapter 14 - The Errors of False Teaching . . 109

Chapter 15 - Money Matters, Or Does It? . . 115

Chapter 16 - The Man of God. . . . 125

Chapter 17 - The Great God 133

Chapter 18 - The Value of Proclamation . . 141

Chapter 19 - Making a Man of God . . . 151

Chapter 20 - I am Saved; Now What? . . 163

Chapter 21- The Value of Perseverance . . 173

Chapter 22 - The Value of Peril . . . 185

Chapter 23 - The Value of Preaching	. . .	197
Chapter 24 - Personal Inspection	. . .	209
Chapter 25 - The Value of Your Presence	. .	217
Chapter 26 - An Introduction to Titus	. .	229
Chapter 27 - The Qualifications of a Pastor	. .	237
Chapter 28 - Dealing with Gainsayers	. .	247
Chapter 29 - Dealing with Old People	. .	257
Chapter 30 - Dealing with Young Ladies	. .	263
Chapter 31 - Dealing with Young Men	. .	271
Chapter 32 - Dealing with Servants	. . .	277
Chapter 33 - The Grace of God	. . .	283
Chapter 34 - Submission and Superiority	. .	293
Chapter 35 - A Concentration on Salvation	. .	301
Chapter 36 - True and False Teaching	. .	309
Chapter 37 - Concluding Remarks	. . .	317

CHAPTER ONE

The Secure Message of the Pastor

I Timothy 1:1-2

This is the first letter that Paul wrote his pastor friend Timothy. Timothy was a pastor who was very gifted, but if Timothy had a weakness, it was the fact that he was timid (cf. II Timothy 1:6-7). Timothy was a man who had to be challenged to stir up the gift that was in him. Naturally, Timothy possessed the spirit of fear.

This element is seen in the opening chapter of I Timothy as well. Paul has to plead with Timothy to stay at Ephesus and face opposition. He has to challenge Timothy to confront those who are preaching false doctrine. It is safe for us to say that Timothy by nature was timid.

Now if there is one thing that will help a pastor get over his timidity, it is the fact that he preaches a message with authority. If the pastor's message was only fables, it would be open to debate (v. 4), but we do not preach a speculation which is to be debated; we preach a divine message which is to be declared. We have the very person of God behind what we say, and there is security in that.

The Message Is Secure Because of Its Source (v. 1a)

Paul and Timothy were intimate friends. As Paul will say in verse 2, there was a father-son relationship that existed between them. Timothy, however, needs to know that this letter is not a friendly, confidential chat. This letter rises above the purely human level. Though the writer is a friend, the writer is also an apostle of Jesus Christ.

Now to be sure, the word *apostle* is frequently used in the Bible of any gospel messenger. There is a sense in which anyone who preaches the gospel is a "sent one." In the Bible, Barnabas, Epaphroditus, Apollos, Silas, and Timothy himself are all called apostles. So, there is a sense in which the word *apostle* is used non-technically in the Bible.

There is also, however, a restricted sense. And that is the way the Apostle Paul is using the word here. When the word *apostle* is used in its technical, restricted sense, there are some things that are true of an apostle.

First, an apostle must have been chosen, called, and sent directly by Christ Himself (Luke 6:13). These twelve who the Bible calls "apostles" were men directly chosen by Jesus. And indeed, when Paul argues for his apostleship in the book of Galatians, he mentions the fact that he received a revelation of and from Jesus (Galatians 1:16). So, Paul, just as certainly as the other twelve, saw Jesus and received His commission directly from the Lord (I Corinthians 15:5-8). Just as the risen Christ was seen by Peter and the rest of the twelve, so he was seen by Paul.

Now once a man had seen the risen Lord, and had been called to be an apostle by that risen Lord, the Lord confirmed that calling with signs and wonders (II Cor-

The Secure Message of the Pastor

inthians 12:12). Signs and wonders were those supernatural displays which accompanied the apostles. Paul wrought those signs and wonders among the Corinthians.

The reason for this was so that men would understand that the apostles had a special endowment of the Holy Spirit which normal people do not possess. And thus, in a sense in which it could be said of no other church-age saint, these men spoke the Word of God. Their voice was God's voice (I Corinthians 2:10-13). The apostles were given truth in a way no other Christian was given it. These men spoke the very word of God.

And thus when Paul says he is an apostle of Jesus Christ, he means that he received his commission directly from Christ, and he means that the word he speaks is the very word of Jesus Christ. He is saying under the inspiration of the Holy Spirit the very things in the very words that Jesus would say.

And lest there be any doubt, Paul intensifies the idea of authority by adding the phrase "by the commandment of God." Paul was not speaking what he wanted to speak. He was a man under orders. He was a man under the directive of God. Therefore, the very letter that was being delivered to Timothy was nothing less than the inerrant, infallible Word of God. This was not Paul's suggestion to Timothy. This was God's orders for Timothy.

When you understand that the parchment you hold in your hand is nothing less than the very word of God, it will do something to you. It will give you security concerning that which you proclaim. The preacher finds security when he remembers the source of his message.

The Message Is Secure Because of Its Result (vv. 1b-2a)

The message comes from God, and who is God? God is our "Savior", and that's a very significant term. The word was used in the cult of Emperor worship. The term in Paul's day was frequently applied to Nero. Paul lets Timothy know unequivocally that Nero is not our Savior. Our Savior is God.

Now let's get more specific. In Paul's mind, who was it that saved sinners? Christ Jesus came into the world to save sinners (v. 15). In the mind of Paul, Christ Jesus was the Savior. Well, in verse one, he says that God is the Savior. How do you reconcile that? You reconcile that by seeing Jesus Christ as God. God is our Savior, and God is Jesus Christ. Therefore, Jesus Christ who is God is our Savior.

Paul further clarifies this at the end of verse one. Our hope is in the Lord Jesus Christ. This is no slender proof that Paul believed in the deity of Jesus. The Greek word *kai* frequently carries with it the idea of "even", and I believe that is the sense here. Paul was an apostle by commandment of God our Savior, even Jesus Christ our hope.

The point is that there is no hope for this life and the next apart from Jesus Christ (Acts 4:12). The hope

The Secure Message of the Pastor

of salvation is found in only one name, and that name is the Lord Jesus Christ. There is no hope, no salvation, apart from Him.

Therefore, the message which we hold in our hands is dynamite. It is dynamite not only because it came from God. It is dynamite because it is the only message that saves men's souls and gives them hope. It is dynamite because of what it produces.

Why was Paul writing to Timothy? How could Timothy understand what was being written? The only way that Paul could give Timothy divine orders and Timothy comprehend them is for Timothy to be born again. The only reason that any of this makes any sense at all is because Timothy is in the faith.

The only reason that Timothy and Paul had a relationship, the only reason that any of this makes any sense, is because Paul preached a message of hope and Timothy believed it. When Timothy placed his trust in the Gospel, when Timothy entered the faith, he was born again (I Corinthians 4:15). When we preach the Gospel and men believe it, they are born again. The privilege is ours to beget men through the gospel. We impart life to them through the Gospel.

Timothy owed his spiritual life to Paul who preached the message of salvation, the message of hope. The fraternity that these men had, the relationship that they enjoyed, is attributable to nothing less than the common faith they shared, the common life that they possessed. This is reason for preaching the gospel (cf. I John 1:3).

Paul tells us in II Corinthians 6:14 that righteousness has no fellowship with unrighteousness. How do we remedy that situation? We remedy it by preaching the Gospel, for when men believe the Gospel, fellowship is established. We declare the Gospel in order that people may have fellowship with us. Fellowship among individuals is found when they share common fellowship with the Father and with His Son Jesus Christ.

The message which we preach is the message which results in salvation. The message which we preach is the message which results in hope. The message which we preach is the message which results in life. The message which we preach is the message which results in fellowship. Therefore, we are secure in our message. We are secure because we know what this message can do.

The Message Is Secure Because of Its Sustaining Power (v. 2b)

If a person takes this message from God and believes it and becomes properly related to God our Father and Jesus Christ our Lord, what is available to that person? The person who has God the Father, and the person who has the Lord Jesus Christ, has at least three things available to him: grace, mercy, and peace.

Let's begin with mercy. Mercy is pardon for the past. A phrase that we use frequently is the phrase "Pardon me." If we commit a tactical error, we will look at our neighbor and say, "Pardon me." But you understand that when the offended party is no one less than a holy God, and the offending party is no one less than a totally vile

The Secure Message of the Pastor   13

man, the phrase "Pardon me" takes on a whole new dimension. In this scenario, pardon is no small task.

Yet this is exactly what God does. He takes every vile act, every vile attitude, and every vile thought and pardons it. The present could not be effectively lived, nor could the future be effectively faced, if the past had not been effectively dealt with. This is what makes the term *mercy* so glorious. God has so effectively dealt with the past that it does not have to be remembered any longer. That's mercy.

Another word used here is *peace*. And the word *peace* speaks of serenity in the present. To be sure there is a peace with God in the sense which the enmity that existed between me and God has been ended. But peace goes much further than that. There is not merely peace with God; there is the peace of God which Paul says in Philippians surpasses understanding. There is peace that doesn't make sense. There is given to the Christian the ability to keep his head when it seems so impossible to do so. We live in a world that is extremely uptight, but for the believer there is serenity for the present. There is peace.

Then Paul mentions grace. If mercy is pardon for the past, and peace is serenity for the present, grace is strength for the future. God not only forgave your past, and gives you peace today, but God also will help you with tomorrow (cf. II Corinthians 12:7-9). God will not eradicate all your trouble, but He will give you the grace to deal with it. God's grace is sufficient for thee.

So the message which we preach is nothing to be

timid about. It is a message which comes from God. It is a message which changes men's lives. It is a message which helps men exist. Is it no wonder that Paul challenged Timothy to hang in there at Ephesus and preach it, rebuking those who are preaching something else? According to verse eleven, this glorious gospel has been committed to our trust. What are we doing with it? Are we ashamed of it? If so, why?

CHAPTER TWO

The Real Gospel

I Timothy 1:3-11

As we begin the main body of I Timothy, we do not have to wait to find out what Paul felt was the most pressing need with regard to his pastor friend. Timothy should by all means stay on duty at Ephesus in order to continue the battle for the truth. It is not merely that the apostle wants the pastor to stay in town. He wants the pastor to stay in town in order that he might contend for the truth. There is no virtue of a pastor staying in a post if he is not going to use that post to straighten out what is wrong.

So specifically, Timothy was to stay on in Ephesus with the purpose of charging certain individuals to teach no other doctrine. Now the very fact that this command was given implies that there were certain individuals who were teaching other doctrine. There is in fact those who teach another gospel (Galatians 1:6-7). There are some people who are eager to embrace that which is new and different (Acts 17:21). We find this tendency at times on the college or seminary campus, where minds having begun a systematic study of the old faith run off into something new and fanciful. Such people, Paul tells Timothy, must be commanded to desist. And the word *charge* is a military term which means "to pass commands from one to another."

So, already there was a Christian body of doctrine.

15

And already some were deviating from that doctrine. And Timothy was told to tell them to stop it.

Now the question might be asked, "Why get in an uproar about false teachers?" Why should we even bother with people who are preaching something else? Why don't we just preach our message and leave them alone? Paul in this passage gives us three reasons why not only the right must be proclaimed, but the wrong must be confronted.

Because the True Gospel Has Superior Content (vv. 3-4)

Wrong preaching comes from wrong thinking. Preachers begin to devote themselves to things which are not profitable. And this is a very dangerous fad. These preachers began to devote their minds to fables and endless genealogies. The expression "fables and endless genealogies" is describing one thing, not two. It is not that Paul is thinking of fables, on the one hand, and endless genealogies on the other. No, the material content of these preachers was genealogical narratives which were largely fictitious.

In Titus 1:14, Paul says that these fables were Jewish fables. And indeed, if you look into works like the Jewish book of Jubilees, you will find a lot of mythical history based on the Old Testament. Based on some hint supplied by the Old Testament, some rabbis would take a name from a genealogy and expand it into a nice story. Even today you will hear certain preachers say "I picture

The Real Gospel   17

Ole So-and-So", and they'll name a Bible character, "doing this and that", and they'll tell you something that is not even close to being found in the text.

That's what these individuals were doing. They were mixing truth and error. And many times the addition became the basis for the appeal. The fanciful story supplied by the preacher became the basis for motivation. But when a preacher adds fiction for theatrical effect, for gross enjoyment, intoxicating thrill, or the satisfaction of curiosity, that preacher has tampered with the very essence of the inspired record. God's Word was not given in order that the public might be entertained with our embellishment of it.

It is clearly obvious that such a preaching style only leads to further questions. And it is not our job primarily to raise questions; it is our job to answer them. And the way we answer the questions of men is by sticking to that which God has entrusted to us.

The word here translated "edifying" is the normal word for stewardship elsewhere in the Bible. A steward is one who manages another's goods. And that's what the preacher does with the Bible. A preacher is a steward of the text of Scripture (I Corinthians 4:1-2). And to that stewardship, he must remain faithful. A pastor is an administrator and dispenser of spiritual treasures. He has the godly stewardship of the faith once-for-all delivered to the saints. He can't waste his time with fanciful make-believe. He must preach the Bible. Paul tells Timothy to tell these men to desist with fables and myths and get back to the Scripture. It has superior content.

Because the True Gospel Reveals a Superior Motive (vv. 5-7)

The purpose of sticking with the Bible, the purpose of keeping this commandment, is that it reveals one's love for the people of God. When these false teachers get away from the Bible, they reveal a lack of love for people. And in revealing that they do not love people, they reveal that their character is deficient.

Love comes out of a pure heart. The "heart" in the Bible speaks of a man's moral affections. Our moral affections ought to be pure. Jesus reserved a special promise for those who were pure in heart. Love for people reveals a pure heart.

Love for people also reveals a good conscience. The word translated "conscience" literally means co-knowledge. And so, when the Bible speaks of a good conscience, it means that the inner voice inside is a repetition of God's voice. Some people's inner voices cannot do this because, as Paul says in 4:2, their consciences are seared. But if you love people, you reveal that your inner voice is echoing the voice of God.

Then Paul says that if you love people, you reveal that you have an unhypocritical faith. Some people fake Christianity, but their hypocrisy with regard to the faith manifests itself in a lack of love for believers. This was true of these false teachers.

So these preachers turned away from the truth of the Bible, and in so doing revealed a lack of love for their people, which in turn revealed a deficient character. And

The Real Gospel   19

so when preachers turn away from the Bible, sad results follow. These preachers have turned away from the goal of helping and loving people. They never reach this destination because they have turned aside and have taken a wrong turn. The pulpit time is merely comprised of a bunch of jangling which is vain. And the very fact that this jangling is called vain, reveals that it does not help anybody. It is vain and empty preaching.

Now deep down in their hearts, these men may even desire to be teachers of the Word. But they did not understand what they were preaching. They failed to understand the very topics on which they lectured with such cock-sureness. These men have no grasp of the sacred text, and thus when they speak, their words are meaningless to themselves and to others. If you don't even understand what you are proclaiming, how are other people going to understand it? Such endeavors clearly reveal a lack of love. Sticking with the true Gospel reveals a superior motive.

Because the True Gospel Produces a Superior Result (vv. 8-11)

The Bible is only profitable provided you make Biblical use of it. Any and all Bible study is not profitable. Preaching is an excellent thing, but not all preaching. It is an excellent thing provided somebody knows how to preach. When you use the Bible, you have to use it for its intended purpose. You can't use the Bible as a take-off point to say what you want to say. You have to use the Bible as it was intended by God.

Paul uses the Old Testament law as an illustration. The law was not given to people who considered themselves to be righteous. In other words, the law was not given to make people feel good about themselves. The law was given so that people would feel utterly crushed underneath the load of sin. If people already feel they are good and righteous, the law is wasted on them. How can the law be a bridle, if I feel I need no restraint? How can the law be a mirror revealing my dirt, if I feel that I am not dirty? How can the law be my guide, if I feel that I have not lost the way? If people perceived that the law was a vehicle to make them righteous, they missed the whole purpose of why the law was given.

The law was not given to help us be good. The law was given to show us that we are bad. And thus the law was given to the lawless, the disobedient, the ungodly, and the sinner. Lawlessness refers to people who violate the law in action. Disobedience refers to insubordination and refers to people who disobey the law in attitude. Negatively speaking, such people are ungodly; they are against God. Positively speaking, they are sinners; they have missed the goal of their existence by going off in unrighteous behavior.

Paul begins to show how these people are in violation of the Ten Commandments. First, they are unholy and in violation of the first commandment, "Thou shalt have no other gods before me." These people are careless in their duties before God, thus revealing that other people and things have taken the place of God in their lives.

The Real Gospel

Second, they are profane, a violation of the second commandment, "Thou shalt not make unto thee any graven image." A profane person is one who substitutes things for the sacred, thus profaning the sacred. For example, in Hebrews 12:16, Esau is called profane because he sold his birthright (something spiritual) for a bowl of pottage (something temporal). When he exchanged the physical for the spiritual, he in essence made an image of that pottage. He was profane. In addition, the Ten Commandments said that the Sabbath day was to be kept holy; it was not to be profaned.

Third, Paul mentions murderers of fathers and murderers of mothers. This is, of course, a flagrant violation of the third commandment, "Honor your father and mother." Moreover, the Mosaic Law prescribed the death penalty for anyone who would strike their parents (Exodus 21:15). If the striking of parents incurred the death penalty, how much more the striking with a destructive blow.

Fourth, the law was intended for manslayers. Of course, this is a violation of the commandment, "Thou shalt not kill." The reference is to anyone who wrongfully takes the life of another.

Fifth, the law was intended for whoremongers, for those who defile themselves with mankind. This clearly refers to those who trespass the commandment, "You shall not commit adultery." This command, of course, is very general; it encompasses all whoredom. And it guards against becoming very perverse; it stops sodomy.

Sixth, the law was instituted for mensteelers. The

word is found only here in the New Testament, but the Greeks used it of slave dealers, and then by extension to all kidnapping. This sin, of course, is a flagrant violation of the commandment, "Thou shalt not steal." Obviously, the Bible took the crime of stealing men very seriously (Exodus 21:16).

Seventh, the law was made for liars, for perjured persons. The apostle obviously has in mind the commandment, "Thou shalt not bear false witness against thy neighbor." And when we remember that perjury was often committed with the view of taking another's property, the final commandment is also included here, "Thou shalt not covet."

The point that Paul is making is that the law was laid down for whatever is laid against sound doctrine. The law was laid down for anything that did not promote spiritual health. The only person for whom the law was not laid down was the person who saw himself as righteous.

So the law demanded that a man keep the whole law. It also declared that a man cannot keep the whole law. Hence, the law revealed man's condition as being utterly lost, thoroughly sinful. The law was meant to drive men to the glorious Gospel of the blessed God. In verse 15, you will notice that Christ Jesus came into the world to save sinners, and therefore the only people who can be benefited by the Gospel are those who see themselves as sinful. This was the whole purpose of the law, to convince men of their sinfulness. The law was our schoolmaster to bring us to Christ.

The Real Gospel

Thus, it is very significant that Paul refers to the glorious Gospel as coming from the blessed God. God is absolute in His perfection; He is perfectly complete. Because God is absolute perfection, He is perfectly self-sufficient. He resides in a state of uninterrupted rest. He is the blessed God.

By contrast, we are turbulently sinful. And the only way this dilemma can be solved is by turning to the blessed God. The only way we can turn to the blessed God is through the glorious Gospel. This glorious Gospel that communicates the blessedness of God to man is committed to our trust. Therefore, we must proclaim it and rebuke anything else that is being proclaimed, for only this message can rescue men from sin and communicate to them the blessedness.

CHAPTER THREE

How the Gospel Fortifies the Pastor

I Timothy 1:12-20

At first, it may appear that Paul has deviated from his argument, but careful examination will reveal that this section is crucial to his argument. If the Gospel can change Paul, the chiefest of sinners, into an apostle of Jesus Christ, then certainly there is no limit to what the Gospel can do. It's transforming power is clearly evident in the Apostle Paul's life. If, then, Timothy argues that he cannot do what the Apostle Paul is asking, and that this stand is beyond his abilities, Timothy is out of touch with reality. The preacher should be assured of the Gospel because he knows what it has done in his own life personally.

Gratitude for the Gospel (v. 12)

Paul is known for frequent outbursts of thanksgiving. These typical exclamations occur because Paul never ceased to marvel at the Gospel. In this particular instance, the praise is for the enabling power of the Gospel. As Paul states here, the Gospel "enabled" him, and the aorist tense points to a past reality. Through the Gospel, God had given Paul strength to engage in the ministry to which he was called.

Paul is simultaneously grateful that God "counted him faithful." The idea here is that of trustworthiness. There is no hint of pride here, for Paul refers to his call-

25

ing as "ministry." The term translates the Greek term *diakonia*, from which we get our word *deacon*. Paul has been called to serve. Moreover, the words "putting me into the ministry" reveal that this ministry was divinely initiated. This was God's idea, not Paul's.

And thus, the enabling, and the favorable judging, and the divine appointment were simultaneous. They all occurred when Paul was converted on the road to Damascus. It was the Gospel that brought all this about. And thus, Paul is deeply grateful for the Gospel. It turned his entire life around. This gratitude will continue to express itself through verse 17. Paul's gratitude will rise higher and higher until it reaches a sublime doxology in that verse.

Grace in the Gospel (vv. 13-17)

This dramatic change in the Apostle Paul's life is highlighted by consideration of what he was before he met Jesus. His pre-Christian state only magnifies how unworthy he is of his apostleship. By his own admission, he was a blasphemer (one who ridicules the name of Christ) and a persecutor (one who attacks the followers of Christ). His life was characterized by inflicting injury on others. The term *injurious* signifies a violent and insolent man, one who possesses a thoroughly objectionable character.

Yet despite his objectionable character, he "obtained mercy." The passive voice reveals that the mercy came from an outside source; there was nothing in Paul personally that merited it. So blinded was Paul by unbe-

How the Gospel Fortifies the Pastor   27

lief, he did not fully realize the extent of his actions. He did what he did "ignorantly", blinded by the "unbelief" that jaundiced his heart. Paul actually thought he was serving God by persecuting Christians (cf. John 16:2). Thus, Paul became the object of God's pity, not God's judgment.

All of this is attributable to the grace of our Lord. The abounding sin of Saul is more than matched by the abounding grace of the Savior. And this grace is no mere abstract concept. It rather becomes an operative and dominant force in Paul's life. Indeed, the Greek preposition *huper* is used to express the super-abundance of this divine grace.

It is only because of this operative grace that faith and love are possible. Paul is only able to exercise faith and love because grace was extended to him. Thus, both faith and love are "in Chirst Jesus." Paul possesses these qualities because of his union with Christ. The Gospel, therefore, has turned him from blaspheming against God to having faith in God, and from being a persecutor against God's children to being in love with them. The Gospel has produced a radical change in Paul personally.

Thus, Paul is convinced that this change can be produced in any sinner. It is faithful saying, that is, a sure word that Christ Jesus came into the world to save sinners. This truth is worthy of acceptance by all people. No sinner should ever doubt the veracity of this truth; it is applicable to all men and worthy of their appropriation.

The fact that Jesus came into the world to save sinners is the very heart of the Gospel. Paul never got away from the fact that Jesus came to save sinners. His own testimony has supported this truth, for Paul viewed himself as the chief of sinners. Paul's humility caused him to see himself as the least of the apostles (I Corinthians 15:9), less than least of all saints (Ephesians 3:8), and the chiefest of sinners. His own life revealed to himself and others just how deep the mercy of God runs.

This mercy that Paul obtained demonstrates just how patient God can be. The word translated "first" in verse 16 is the same word translated "chief" in verse 15. By reaching the superlative sinner, Jesus Christ shows His superlative patience. This long-suffering nature of Christ is designed to be a pattern for centuries to come. The word *pattern* was used of an outline or sketch of an artist. Paul's conversion was meant to serve as a sketch to show people how God would deal with sinners in the future. And those who have believed since Paul's day can equally testify to the patience of Christ.

Those who have experienced such grace can only marvel at it and praise the Lord for it. Thus, verse 17 is an all-absorbing adoration of God. The fact that God gives mercy in the present so that we can have life for eternity (v. 16) reveals that He is the King of all ages. To this immortal, invisible, and all-wise God belongs honor and glory forever and ever. Amen!

Guardianship of the Gospel (vv. 18-20)

If a preacher has a proper gratitude for the Gospel because of his understanding of the rich grace that is in the Gospel, then that preacher will assume the responsibility of guarding the Gospel that has been committed to his trust. This is the charge that has been committed to the pastor. The term translated "charge" was used in military contexts of an urgent obligation. The Gospel is not something to be trifled with. It is an order from our commander-in-chief. And thus, it must be protected at all costs.

The very fact that one is in the ministry at all is due to the eternal decree of God (cf. Ephesians 2:10). Recognizing, therefore, that we are in the ministry because of "the prophecies which went before", we must covenant to stay in the fight for the Gospel. The call of God upon our lives should inspire us for the conflict that lies ahead.

If the pastor is to be successful in this conflict, two things are indispensable. The first is holding on to the faith. The pastor must be doctrinally sound, holding on to the articles of faith with rabid tenacity. Second, the pastor must maintain a good conscience. Thus, a pastor must believe the truth and live in accordance with it. Both his beliefs and his behavior should mirror the Gospel that he proclaims.

Unfortunately, this is not always a given with pastors. Some have "put away" these indispensable qualities of the faith, and the results of have been catastrophic.

When a preacher is guilty of doctrinal or moral failure, shipwreck is inevitable. Paul moves from a military metaphor to a nautical one. The pastor must not only be a good soldier; he must also be a good sailor. When the rudder of truth is discarded, shipwreck is the inevitable result.

This is not merely a theoretical possibility. Paul could point to two men (Hymenaeus and Alexander) who had so erred. These men were not treated lightly. Paul says that he "delivered them unto Satan." This phrase is used in I Corinthians 5:5 to refer to removal from the church. They were put out of the church into the province of Satan.

The purpose of this excommunication is not damnation but reclamation. They were delivered unto Satan in order that they might "learn not to blaspheme." All church discipline should have a remedial aim, not a punitive one. Whenever church discipline departs from the goal of restoration, it violates Scripture. This in no way, however, suggests that church discipline should be avoided. The purity of the Gospel should always be protected.

CHAPTER FOUR

The Importance of Public Prayer

I Timothy 2:1-8

In the first chapter of I Timothy, we have dealt with the message of the Christian worship service; it is the message of the Gospel. Now when we come to chapter two, we deal with the method of the Christian worship service. And the first thing that the Apostle Paul will discuss is prayer. As Paul begins to lay down the organization of the church, the thing that is of primary importance is prayer.

The phrase "first of all" in verse 1 does not refer to the primacy of time, but to the primacy of importance. It is essential at the onset to ensure a noble approach to public worship, and the premier way that this is to be done is by stressing the importance of prayer.

The Elements of Prayer (v. 1a)

When Paul urges Timothy to make prayer an integral part of the worship service, he lists four components of prayer, four things which ought to characterize prayer. The first is specificity. When Paul mentions the word *supplications*, he is talking about asking God for specific needs which are keenly felt. We ask God that this specific illness might be removed. We ask God that this particular disturbing thing might be over-turned. Supplication is asking God to do something in concrete situations of life. Prayer is to be specific.

31

Second, prayer is to be reverent. The word *prayer* is a word that is used to describe a reverent address to deity. The point is that while we have freedom of access to the throne of grace, we must never take for granted that we are talking to God. When we pray, we say, "Our Father, who is in Heaven, hallowed be your name." God is to be addressed reverently; after all, it is prayer.

Third, prayer is to be intercessory. The word *intercession* comes from a root which means "falling in with." While praying, we are to fall in with the interests of other people. We sometimes confine prayer to our own narrow interests, but as Paul will say later, prayer is to be made for all men. Thus, prayer is to be intercessory. We are to plead in the interests of others.

Finally, prayer is to be thankful. It is sad, but many of our prayers are so concerned with obtaining things from God that we have never spend time thanking God for what He has already done for us and others. Even though thankfulness is an element that we have neglected in prayer, Paul argues that it be done. Thankfulness is an integral part of prayer.

The Objects of Prayer (vv. 1b-7)

As we have hinted at earlier, prayer is not to be confined to our own narrow interests. Prayer is to be made for others. Notice two specific ways in which we can pray for others.

Pray for the State (vv. 1b-2)

When we go to pray for all men, we should specifically pray for those who are part of the ruling class. We have to be reminded to do this because throughout church history, many times those in government have been hostile to the cause of Christ. Because this is true, we allow animosity to build in our hearts for those in authority, and we stop praying for them.

But the Christian attitude towards the state is of utmost importance. It is not a matter of whether the state is perverted or not. Regardless, it should be made the object of prayer. Christian citizens can influence the course of national affairs by praying for those in government. And this is a fact often forgotten except in times of special crisis. But habitually the church should pray for those leading in the affairs of state.

The reason that we are to do this is in order that we might lead a quiet and peaceable life. Through our prayers, government can achieve conditions of peace and security. There should be a quietness and tranquility, a calmness and serenity, in social affairs. Our prayers for those in government can help achieve this.

We want this to be achieved because it enables us to live our Christian life unhindered. We do not want oppression from the state concerning the faith. We want to be able to live godly and honestly without fear of government reprisal. We want to be sincere, godly Christians, and this can best be done when an atmosphere of peace and serenity prevails. Therefore, we must pray for the state constantly.

Pray for Men's Salvation (vv. 3-7)

Whenever you and I engage in prayer, we are doing something which is good. We never have to wonder whether prayer is the wrong thing to do. Prayer is always the right thing to do. Prayer is always something which is acceptable in the sight of God. We as Christians should want to do things that are good and acceptable in the sight of God. Therefore, we should pray.

Now when we pray, as we have already stated, we must remember to whom we pray. We pray to God. God is our Savior, and since God is a Savior, it is in the very nature of God to save. Thus, one reason that we know we can pray for all men (v. 1) is because God wants all men to be saved. God has a constant mercy towards all, irrespective of race, color, condition, or status. We sometimes tend to be exclusive in our prayers. The nature of God knows nothing of such exclusiveness. God wants all men to be saved, and therefore we ought to pray for all men. God's universal compassion ought to be our compassion. So intercession for all men is justified on the grounds that God is willing to save all.

Now some Calvinists have argued that the word *save* should be taken in its lesser sense of "preserve" or "protect." They would argue based on verse 2 that God wants to preserve and protect all men from lawless misrule. God wants to save all men from tyrannical governments. But the passage as a whole seems too theological to be so interpreted, and the concluding part of the verse adds the phrase that God wants all men "to come

The Importance of Public Prayer 35

to a knowledge of the truth." This phrase accords much better with spiritual salvation than it does with natural preservation. The point cannot be denied, therefore, that God wants all to be saved, and therefore we are to pray for all men's salvation.

When men are saved, they are saved by coming to a knowledge of the truth. Two things in the Bible are called truth. Thy word is truth (John 17:17), and Jesus said, "I am the truth" (John 14:6). So men are saved by coming to know Jesus through the Bible. They are saved by a knowledge of the truth. The only way that a man can be saved is through the revelation of God in Christ.

There are not many ways of salvation, for there are not many gods. There is only one God, and hence there is only one way of salvation. There is only one way that the enmity of God and man can be alleviated. There is only one form of mediation. Indeed, there is only one mediator. There is only one person that can settle the dispute between God and man, and that mediator is the man Christ Jesus. At this point, Christianity is very exclusive. There is only one God, and that one God has established only one way of salvation. And that one way of salvation is Jesus Christ (cf. Acts 4:12).

How did Jesus mediate the dispute? How did Jesus accomplish salvation? He did so by giving Himself a ransom for all. Notice the progression. We are to pray for all men (v. 1). We are to do so because God wants all men to be saved (v. 4). And God proved that He wanted all men to be saved when He sent Jesus to give His life a ransom for all (v. 6).

The word used here of the atonement is *ransom.* Jesus used this word Himself (Mark 10:45). Christ paid the price by which you and I can be free. And two different prepositions are used in I Timothy to express this thought. The first is the preposition *anti,* which means "instead of." The second preposition is *huper* meaning "on behalf of." Christ paid the ransom price on behalf of and in the place of all. Christ paid the price whereby freedom can be granted to all men. This was God's plan before the foundation of the world, and God bore witness to that plan when He sent Jesus Christ into history in the fullness of time to accomplish redemption.

It is true that not all men enjoy that freedom. For the freedom to be enjoyed, the ransom must be personally appropriated. The point is that there is only one thing that limits salvation, and it is the unbelief of men. Christ has paid the ransom for all, because He wants all men to be saved, and that is why He commands us to pray for all men.

But it goes even further than that. God not only paid the price, but He ordained certain men to go and preach that news of redemption. The stress here is on the divine origin of Paul's call. He had not appointed himself to so great and hazardous a task. That task was laid upon him by God. Paul never ceased to wonder at it. Certain ones at Ephesus may have wondered if indeed Paul had been ordained to do this. Certainly Timothy's ministry would be in doubt if Paul's ministry was in doubt. But when it came to Paul's call to preach, he was never more sure of anything. That was the truth in Christ; it was no lie.

The Importance of Public Prayer

The reason that Paul had to state it so emphatically was because nothing less than the veracity of the Gentile mission was at stake. Paul's call to be an apostle was a very special call; it was a call to the Gentiles (cf. Acts 9:15). The very fact that the Gentiles are mentioned first shows where God's priority was with Paul. He was a special apostle to the Gentiles. These were the people that he was to teach.

Now, of course, many Jews doubted whether God would or could save the Gentiles. But God says pray for all men because I want all men to be saved. I have given my life a ransom for all men. I have ordained certain preachers to go to those who you would think the most unlikely candidates for salvation. If there is only one God (v. 5), then He must be the God of everyone (Romans 3:29-30). If these others are to be saved, they have to come to our God, for there is no other god. Therefore, we must pray that men come to this God and preach so that they can come to this God.

When we teach the heathen, we must do so in faith and verity. The word *verity* translates the same word translated "truth" in verse 4. We cannot contextualize the message to fit men's culture. We have to tell them the truth, for the truth is the only thing that can save them. As we proclaim the truth, we have the faith that the truth will liberate. We have the hope that men will embrace it and be saved. This entire hope in the effectiveness of the Gospel through our preaching is proven by our prayers. We need to pray for men's salvation.

The Method of Prayer (v. 8)

A key to understanding verse 8 is to remember that we are talking about public worship service. Concerning the prayers of public worship, Paul makes his apostolic will known. He wills that men pray everywhere, lifting up holy hands, without wrath or doubting. Now there are three things that we can glean from this admonition.

Public Prayer Is for Men, not Females (v. 8a)

When Paul mentions men in verse 8, he is contrasting them with females (v. 9). And specifically in the context of females, the admonition for them is silence (vv. 11-12). Now this does not mean that women cannot pray in church. It does mean, however, that they should pray like Hannah. "She spoke in her heart; only her lips moved, but her voice was not heard." We are not saying that women cannot pray when we break up into prayer groups. We are saying that women should not lead men in prayer. The public prayer of the worship service is to be made by men, not females.

Public Prayer Is for Men who Are Forgiven (v. 8b)

A man can pray in any church provided that his hands are holy. His hands must be unpolluted from previous crimes. Specifically, Paul says that he cannot be harboring wrath. He cannot have a settled indignation against someone. Such wrath makes prayer unacceptable. How can you pray for all men, if there are some

The Importance of Public Prayer   39

men with whom you have unsettled differences? How can you intercede for those with whom you are angry? Therefore, public prayer is for men who have been forgiven from their malice.

Public Prayer Is for Men of Faith (v. 8c)

There are many postures of prayer mentioned in the Bible. Some men stood. Some men bowed their heads. Some men lifted their eyes heavenward. Some men knelt. Some men fell down with their face on the ground. But here the posture is one of lifting holy hands. The lifting up of hands symbolizes that the one who is praying is expecting to receive something from God. He is dependent upon God. His attitude is one of humble expectancy. In a word, Paul says that he prays without doubting. I remember Dr. Lee Roberson praying with his hands raised, and it did something for me. From time to time, I, in public worship, pray with my hands raised. I want something from God, and I believe that God can give it to me. So the man who prays in public worship must pray in forgiveness, but also pray in faith, believing and trusting in God.

What a great variety our prayers can take. They can be supplications, prayers, intercessions, or giving of thanks. What a great scope our prayers can take. We can pray for the highest government officials; we can pray for all living men. Therefore, we had better be the kind of men whose prayers are answered. That necessitates that we pray as clean individuals and as expectant individuals. Prayer is so important to the life of a church. Let's make sure our prayer services are right.

CHAPTER FIVE

The Role of Women in Public Worship

I Timothy 2:9-15

The phrase "in like manner" shows that Paul is continuing his discussion about public worship. In verse 8, we saw that there is a particular way that men are to conduct themselves in public worship. They are to have holy hands, and they are to come hoping to receive something from the Lord. But if there is a proper way for men to come to church, there is also a proper way for women to come to church. And that is what Paul is discussing here, the role of women in public worship.

Their Attitude toward Apparel (vv. 9-10)

When women come to church, they are to adorn themselves in modest apparel. The word here translated "modest" comes from the Geek root *kosmos*, which refers to the order and arrangement of the universe. In other words, the clothing of a woman ought to be orderly. The way clothing is orderly is by being modest. The word translated "apparel" literally means "something let down." In other words, clothing is orderly and proper when it is modest. Clothing fulfills its intended function when it conceals, not when it reveals. We often speak of revealing clothes. Clothes were never meant to reveal. They were meant to conceal.

Now let's be honest with ourselves. When a woman comes to church, and she is not dressed modestly, attention is immediately directed toward that woman. The goal of public worship is not to get people to look at man; it is to get people to look at God. Therefore, when a woman dresses immodestly, she is taking the attention that should be upon God and directing that attention upon herself. She has misused and abused the entire purpose for which clothes were given.

Paul says here that a Christian lady ought to be dressed with shamefacedness. In other words, the very thought of crossing the line of impropriety ought to make a woman blush with shame. She ought to shrink from the very thought of trespassing the boundaries of propriety. She ought to have a proper reserve about herself.

This at its core is simply a matter of common sense. Paul says that a woman ought to dress with sobriety. Women ought to have a soundness of mind. When some women get ready for church, they simply do not use their God-given brains. Some don't dress seriously when they come to church. Their dress does not look like church dress at all; it is characterized by levity and frivolity. Paul here is calling for sanity, when it comes to the appearance of Christian women.

Now in addition to immodesty, women also distract from the worship of God when their clothing is extravagant. Now there are three specific ways that women can become extravagant in their dress. And the first area has to do with their hair. In Bible times, women would braid their hair and then put in all kinds of fancy ribbons and bows in it. These ribbons and bows would be attached

The Role of Women in Public Worship 43

with pins that were very dazzling. Sometimes these pins would be shaped like animals, or human hands, or female figurines. Women would try to outdo each other with these ornaments. The point is that if someone is paying more attention to your hair, than they are the worship of God, you have crossed the line.

The second area where women can cross the line in extravagance is jewelry. Paul is not saying that women can't wear jewelry; he is saying that the wearing of gold and pearls can many times cross over into the realm of extravagance and be a distraction in worship.

The same is true of costly array. A lady of God should not desire flashy clothes simply for the sake of showmanship, so that on Sunday she will be the topic of conversation. When we gather together on Sunday to worship God, we have not come to discuss what a lady is wearing or what she is not wearing. Our Christian sister was never meant to be the topic of conversation. God is meant to be the topic of conversation. Therefore, dear sister, when you come to church, you ought to dress in such a way that people are not even looking at you; they are looking at God. This demands modesty and lack of extravagance. Ladies should have a right attitude toward apparel.

It is sad but today more people spend time worrying about what they are going to wear to church than about the attitude of their heart while they are there. Christian women are women who profess to be godly. Should not their attire, therefore, reflect that profession? Shouldn't God's women be more concerned about doing good works than wearing good clothes? Doesn't selfless service for others do more to enhance a woman's appearance than attire does anyway? In short, a woman's adornment does not lie in what clothes she puts on; it lies in what service she gives out (I Peter 3:3-4). True beauty is not to be found on the outside; it is to be found on the inside. Women need to have the right attitude toward apparel.

A Right Attitude toward Authority (vv. 11-14)

Paul says that when it comes to public worship, women ought to learn in silence. This is a matter of heart, a matter of attitude. If a woman comes to church with the attitude that she is going to straighten things out, she violates the Word of God. Her attitude in coming to church is not to be one of instructing others; her attitude is to be one of being instructed. She is to listen quietly. This is done by assuming an attitude of submission. The word translated "submission" literally means "to arrange under." When a woman comes to church, she is to arrange herself not above men, but under them. She has come to learn from them. You can't learn when your mouth is always open. So, Paul instructs them to arrange themselves under men, keeping their mouths silent to learn.

Thus, when Paul says that a woman is not permitted to teach, he is by no means implying that women do not have the gift of teaching. Indeed, in other passages, Paul specifically tells older women to teach younger women. This is not a blanket statement that women are never to

The Role of Women in Public Worship   45

teach. It is, however, a blanket statement about women teaching in the public worship service of the church. A woman is never to usurp authority over a man. In this particular arena, she is to be silent. A woman should not exercise authority over a man by lecturing him in public worship. Never in a public worship setting should a woman try to lay down the law to a man. She is to have a proper attitude toward authority.

Because this is an area that is so frequently rebelled against, Paul has to remind us of two particular historical facts. The first is that Adam was made before Eve. Man's priority in creation puts him in a position of superiority as far as authority is concerned. Indeed, the reason why Eve was made was that she was made for Adam. God made the woman for him (Genesiss 2:18). This is not limited to Adam and Eve (I Corinthians 11:7-9). For centuries, women have been fighting against this, but it does not change the Word of God one bit. God made Eve for Adam, to follow Him. And to reverse that order and have man follow woman is wrong.

The second historical fact that Paul would bring up is the Fall. Paul references the Fall to pinpoint Eve's deception. When Eve left the protective umbrella of her husband's authority, and tried to be the spiritual head of that home by boycotting her husband's advice, she was deceived. Instead of following, Eve chose to lead. It got her and her husband in trouble. She put her husband in the precarious position of choosing between fellowship with God and fellowship with her. Adam plunged the whole race into sin willfully because Eve initially got out of her role as a woman. So really you can trace the abiding state of transgression that we are all in back to a lack of spousal submission. Now we are not excusing Adam, and Paul condemns Adam in Romans 5 without even mentioning Eve. But the argument here is that Eve started the ball rolling when she removed herself from her husband's authority. Public church gatherings can become very turbulent when women do not know their rightful place. We need Christian women who have a right attitude toward authority.

A Right Attitude toward Attitude (v. 15)

Verse 15 is the most controversial passage in the pastoral epistles. There has been no small discussion about it. There are four major interpretations, and we will examine them all to hopefully arrive at a proper interpretation. The key to interpreting the verse is the last half of it. Whatever it means for women to be saved in childbearing, it comes about if women continue in faith, and charity, and holiness with sobriety.

Some believe this verse refers to women getting safely through the child-bearing process. Even though labor is part of the curse, God promises women that they will get through it safely. The problem with this interpretation is that it does not accord well with the facts. There are women who have been faithful, loving, and holy, and they have not gone through child-birth safely. On the other hand, there have been faithless, hateful, unholy women who have delivered children quite safely. There is no evidence

The Role of Women in Public Worship   47

that the character of the mom directly relates to safety in childbirth.

The second interpretation is that we take the word *save* in the spiritual sense, interpreting the verse to mean that women will be saved by having children who are faithful, loving, and holy. Once again, this is inconceivable, especially when you look at the rest of the Bible. A person's spiritual state is not conditioned upon the spiritual state of their children. There are some godly people with ungodly kids, and some ungodly parents with godly kids. If my personal salvation is contingent upon the spirituality of my children, then salvation is something which is earned and merited. Such a thought could never be.

The third interpretation is that the child-bearing here refers to the birth of the Messiah. If this is what Paul meant to say, that we are saved through the birth of one man, the Messiah, he could not have found a more obscure way of saying it. Moreover, if this is what Paul had in mind, you would expect a definite article with the word *childbearing*. Women are saved through the childbearing. But Paul does not use a definite article, implying that it is the total process of child-birth which is under discussion, not one particular birth.

That brings us to the fourth interpretation, which I feel is the right one. The thought is that even though the woman has removed herself from her husband's authority, even though she initiated the fall of mankind, even though she was cursed with pain in childbirth, she can still be saved. Peter, for example, spends six verses telling women that they have to be submissive, but this has nothing at all to do with inferiority when it comes to salvation. Concerning the grace of life, we are heirs together (I Peter 3:1-7). The submissive role of the wife has nothing to do with her essence. God has provided for her salvation just as much as He has provided for man's salvation.

The evidence of this conversion is a continuation in faithfulness, charity, holiness, and self-control. She continues in all of this in spite of the fact that she has to go through labor. I am convinced that if I had to go through childbirth, I would have already lost my salvation. If she can go through all the pain of childbirth and still be a faithful, loving, holy, self-controlled woman, there is no greater evidence of salvation.

A woman should never think that because God has placed her in a role of submission this means inferiority. She is no more inferior to her husband than Christ is inferior to the Heavenly Father. It has nothing to do with essence; it has everything to do with authority. If she accepts this, it will do something for her attitude. It will make her happier, her husband happier, and the whole church happier.

CHAPTER SIX

The Office of the Bishop

I Timothy 3:1-7

I Timothy 1, we looked at the message of the Christian church. In I Timothy 2, we looked at the method of the Christian church. Now obviously, if we have a message to proclaim and a method of propriety, then obviously we need men of authority to lead us to this desired end. There is to be ecclesiastical authority in the church. God intends for a local church to have offices and officers.

The first office that he mentions is the office of a bishop. The Greek word is *episcopos,* and it means "overseer." Up until the time of Ignatius, the term always referred to one who exercised oversight in a local church. The term prior to that time never referred to a monarchial episcopacy such as that seen in the Catholic and Episcopalian systems. A bishop was always one who exercised oversight within a local church.

Because the term *bishop* has come to mean in the English language, a person who is over an entire district of churches, Baptists have preferred the term *pastor.* But what we call a pastor is technically called by the Bible "the office of a bishop." While the Bible uses the term *angel,* the term *pastor,* and the term *elder* to amplify our understanding of the office, the office itself is that of a bishop. What does Paul have to say about this office?

49

The Aspiration for the Office (v. 1)

If any man desires the office of a bishop, he desires a good work. Being a pastor is an excellent occupation. This is a fact that many parents need to realize. If your son ever comes home and says, "Mom and Dad, I want to be a pastor", you should not be mortified by that news. If a child desires the office of a bishop, he desires a great profession. What greater job is there in all the world than the job of being a pastor?

Now concerning this choice of profession, the Apostle Paul uses interesting terminology. The first word translated "desire" is the word *oregomai*, which literally means "to stretch oneself out." Hence, the office of the pastorate is one that a man aspires to. He reaches out to take hold of it. This is one of the things that makes the office of a pastor vastly different from the office of a deacon. When it came to the business affairs of the church, the office of deacon, the office sought the man (Acts 6:1-3). But here the exact opposite is true; the man seeks the office.

The second word translated "desire" is the Greek term *epithumeo*, which intimates a very strong internal desire. It is something on which the heart is set. All of this implies a divine calling. God had placed a compulsion in Paul (cf. I Corinthians 9:16). There is nothing else that Paul could do rather than preach the Gospel. That desire to preach or die was placed there by God. Pastoring is not one of several good options. If a man can do anything else other than preach, he should not

The Office of the Bishop

be preaching. With his whole heart he should aspire for the office and reach out and take it.

The Qualifications for the Office (vv. 2-7)

Obviously, the call of God is subjective. When a man says that he is called to pastor, he indeed may not be called. Not everyone who has purported to be called by God has indeed been called by God. Therefore, there must be some objective way whereby the church can judge the validity of such a profession. Hence this list of qualifications is given. Those whom God calls, He qualifies.

Thus, the first thing that is true of a pastor is that he must be blameless. He must be without reproach. This does not mean that a pastor will never be accused of things. Indeed, he will be. But the pastor must never give reason for those accusations to stick. His character must be such that it is not quickly called into question. This is the overall requirement which governs the rest in the list.

The second thing that Paul says must be true of a pastor is that he must be the husband of one wife, literally he must be a one-woman man. What does this mean? There have been three major interpretations throughout the history of the church. The first is that this verse condemns polygamy. Polygamy was widely practiced among the heathen; it still is in certain parts of the globe. Some have taken the verse to mean that the pastor cannot be married to more than one woman simultaneously.

A second interpretation dating all the way back to Tertullian, states that this is a prohibition against second marriages. In other words, the pastor is prohibited, not only from marrying two women simultaneously, but also from marrying them serially. The prohibition then would restrict men who have been divorced and remarried from holding the office of pastor.

A third interpretation goes even further and states that a bishop must exercise strict morality. I believe this is the proper interpretation. As you look at the list as a whole, it discusses the practice of the man. In other words, the pastor is to be a one-woman man, not a ladies' man. I believe that the first two interpretations are encompassed in this, but they do not exhaust it. A pastor who has never been divorced and remarried can still be flirtatious. Such should not be the case. A pastor should only husband one wife.

Third, the pastor must be vigilant. The idea here is that a pastor is not to be superficial. He is to be spiritually deep. His pleasures are not primarily those of the senses, but rather those of the soul. He is to be morally and spiritually earnest. He is to be vigilant in the cause of Christ.

Fourth, the pastor must sober. He is to be self-controlled. He is to be sensible. He is to be a man of a sound mind. He is not to be swayed by sudden impulses over which he exercises no mastery. He should not accept nonsense readily.

Fifth, the pastor must be of good behavior. He must possess an inner moral excellency and an outward orderly

The Office of the Bishop

behavior. His life should be in good moral order. People should be able to say of him that his behavior is good.

Sixth, the pastor is to be given to hospitality. The underlying Greek word literally means "a friend of strangers." This was an especially important requirement in the early church in a day of no motels and no church buildings. Because it has become more feasible to do so, we should not minimize this requirement. All of us should be characterized by having an open-door policy at our homes. This is especially true of pastors.

Seventh, the pastor should be apt to teach. This to me is one requirement where Baptists have seriously dropped the ball in recent days. When Paul gave instructions to Titus about ordination, he said that those who are ordained should be able by sound doctrine to exhort and convince the gainsayers (Titus 1:9). It is sad, but many Jehovah's Witnesses are better schooled in error than our Baptist preachers are in truth. Some pastors are great administrators, but they are terrible teachers. Pastors should be apt to teach.

Eighth, the pastor should not be given to wine. Obviously, this is not talking about wine for medicinal purposes, for Paul will tell Timothy later on to take wine for his stomach's sake. As a beverage, the pastor is to avoid wine. He is not to give himself to it.

Ninth, the pastor should not be a striker. This does not mean he should avoid labor unions. It means the pastor should not be given to blows. He should not be ready to fight with his fists, a spitfire. A pastor should not be a man who is eager to engage in combat.

Tenth, the pastor should not be greedy of filthy lucre. The acquisition of money should not be the chief end of the pastor. In a word, he should not be like Judas Iscariot who was quickly persuaded to compromise spiritual office for financial remuneration. There will come a time in every pastor's ministry when he will have to choose between money and the Master. He cannot be greedy of filthy lucre.

Eleventh, the pastor should be patient. Patience is the positive quality of guarding against striking. A pastor should be gracious, kind, forbearing, considerate, magnanimous, and genial (Titus 3:2). If this is true of all Christians, how much more is it necessary in a pastor? In II Corinthians 10:1, Paul refers to the gentleness and meekness of Christ. Christ exemplifies par excellence this quality. Pastors ought to try to be like Jesus in this regard.

Then twelfth, he cannot be a brawler, that is, he cannot be contentious. He must not only refrain from fighting with his hands; he must refrain from arguing with his lips. He cannot be disputatious and argumentative. With regards to the Gospel, he never flinches, but with regard to his own personal rights, he is willing to flinch.

Thirteen, he is not to be covetous. The Bible tells us in other passages that covetousness is idolatry. It is so easy to make things our God. Obviously, the pastor cannot direct people's attention to God if his eyes are stuck on material possessions. He must refrain from that covetous spirit.

Then fourteen, he must manage his own household

The Office of the Bishop 55

well. This qualification has not always been given the prominence that it deserves. A pastor should be able to govern his children graciously and gravely. Now the principle that is propounded here is universally true. The test as to whether a man is capable of bigger things is his ability to handle smaller things (Matthew 25:21). The potential skill in a larger sphere can only be indicated by similar skill in a lesser sphere. Thus, a man's ability to lead in the church can be observed in the way that this man leads his home. Are his children under control? There is a dignity about home life that the pastor should carefully recognize. And if that pastor does not rule his own house well, he is disqualified from taking care of the church of God.

Fifteen, the pastor must not be a novice. The Greek word *neophyte* literally means "one who is newly planted." If it has only been a short time since this person has been buried in the likeness of Christ's death, if there has been no opportunity to watch growth, then he should not be a pastor. It would seem wise that at least a couple of years should pass before a saved man enters into full-time ministry.

Advancement that comes too quick fosters pride. The Greek word translated "lifted up with pride" is *tuphoo* which literally means "to wrap in smoke." Such a man is under the allusion that he has substance, when he does not. He is in a cloudland of deceit. His rise has given him the impression that he is somebody, but this is a false sense of altitude, and it will make his fall all the more greater.

The devil was given a great office and pride ruined him. He came crashing down. Men who are put into the pastorate too soon will experience that same kind of judgment. They will fall from their office just as the devil did from his. So we must refrain from the temptation of putting a new convert into the pastorate.

Then finally, the pastor is to have a good report of them that are without. In short, the pastor should have a good reputation in the community. He will have to conduct business in the work-a-day world. What impression do the unsaved have of him? Their judgment is of some importance. Worldlings, because their father is the devil, like to slander the believer, especially the leader of the church. The trap into which many pastors fall is that the world will beg them to lower their standards, and then reproach them when they do. The pastor must be careful of the way he conducts himself in front of the unsaved.

CHAPTER SEVEN

The Duties of a Deacon

I Timothy 3:8-13

The earliest allusion we have to deaconing occurs in Acts 6. The appointment of seven men to deacon was mainly practical. A deacon, according to Acts 6:1-4, was to serve tables, and the word there translated "table" is *trapeza*; it refers to a money table. When Jesus went into the temple, he overturned the tables of money. Just as there is an officer to run the church spiritually, so there are officers who handle the finances of the church.

This does not mean that the pastor is indifferent to the financial picture of the church. It certainly does not mean that the pastor cannot call for special offerings on specific occasions, but it does mean that the pastor should never directly handle the money. He should not make the deposits, handle the checkbook, and spend without some type of board guideline. For these matters, we have elected deacons.

Now once again we need to hasten to add that because the function is financial, this does not mean that spirituality is unimportant. Quite the contrary is true. When we are talking about the Lord's money, the men who distribute it must be deeply spiritual. They must be morally equipped just as the pastor is to be morally equipped.

The Heart of the Deacon (vv. 8-10)

The first thing that the Bible says must be true of a deacon is that he must be grave. Now obviously, people who give to a church must feel that there is some thought being given to expenditure. This necessitates that deacons have a certain decorum, a certain propriety of manner. In order to have the respect of the congregation, they must conduct themselves in a respectable way. This does not mean that they never laugh or joke, but it does mean that they treat the matters of the church seriously. They are grave.

Second, they cannot be double-tongued. There are many applications to this, and it is very important when it comes to money that this be true. A deacon cannot talk out of both sides of his mouth. He cannot say one thing to the congregation when in the back of his mind he knows another thing to be true. He cannot communicate one thing to one person and another thing to another. He cannot be guilty of gossip concerning that which is given to the church. In short, the deacon must mean what he says, and say what he means. He cannot be double-tongued.

Third, the deacon is not to be given to much wine. Obviously, when there is a lot of wine in a person, judgment is impaired (Proverbs 31:4-5). Those in leadership should not be given to much wine. It blurs their ability to make right decisions. The judgment of the deacon must be crisp, and therefore much wine is to be avoided.

Then they are not to be greedy of filthy lucre. Since

The Duties of a Deacon 59

deacons are responsible for counting the money, it is very important that greed not be a part of their temperament. The temptation to extract funds for personal use would be great. A deacon should never look at the congregation with dollar signs. He should not be constantly thinking of ways that these people can be pilfered. As we saw from Acts 6, his job is to help people with money, not help himself. He cannot be greedy of filthy lucre.

All of this implies that the deacon must not simply be a man of practical acumen; he must be a man of spiritual convictions. We cannot pick a man to be a deacon simply because he has a good business head. He should have a good business head, but not merely that. With that practical ability must be spirituality. Paul puts it this way: he must hold the mystery of the faith in a pure conscience.

Not everybody understands the faith. It is something which God hides to those who refuse to see. And it is something which is revealed to those with spiritual discernment. A deacon must be among the enlightened. He must know the faith which, to many, is a mysterious thing. And knowing that body of doctrine, he must tenaciously hold to it. The deacon watches himself scrupulously to do all in his power to remain in the closest possible conformity to the faith. In a word, his heart must be right.

Now if that is true, then deacons should be elected only after they have proven themselves. We are not talking here about some kind of examination, but rather a period of probation. A man should be seen in operation in the church for a while before he becomes a deacon. The word here translated "proved" means "to test in the hope of being successful." We are not to put a man under the microscope in hopes that he will fail. Rather, the hope is that he will succeed. And if indeed he does succeed and has been found to be blameless, then let him use the office of a deacon. He is acting like a deacon, so let's give him the office of deacon. His heart is right.

The Home of the Deacon (vv. 11-12)

There has been no small discussion about what verse 11 is talking about. It is clear that the words "must their" are in italics. So literally, the text reads, "Even so wives." And in the Greek, there was no word for "wife." Whenever you wanted to refer to a man's wife, you referred to her as his woman. There just was no word for wife. So even more literally, the text reads, "Even so women." The King James translators understood this to mean the deacons' women, that is, the deacons' wives. And there is much that can be said for this interpretation. It was very likely that a deacon would have to take his wife with him as he visited widows to minister funds. Obviously, that woman would have to be spiritual too.

But the fact that the words "even so" occur, seem to intimate that Paul is referring to another class of servants, female servants. We know from early church writings that there were actually deaconesses; they did jobs for widows which men were unable to do. For example, they would go into widows' homes and bathe them. They would help female candidates prepare for baptism.

The Duties of a Deacon   61

Obviously, there are parts of being a deacon that can-not be performed by men. And there arose a necessity of placing women in charge of these functions. You will notice that there is nothing said about the wife of the pastor. We, therefore, would not expect to find anything about the wife of a deacon. For these reasons, many have felt that deaconesses are under discussion here.

But the ideas are not mutually exclusive. Most of the women who served as deaconesses were the wives of deacons. So the idea may be that if your wife is going to assist you in this office, make sure that certain things are true of her.

First, make sure that she is grave. Just as you must make sure that you approach the office with gravity (v. 8), so she must also. In addition, she cannot be a slan-derer. If it is true that you are not to be double-tongued (v. 8), make sure that she has control of her tongue as well. She is going to see women who are destitute and in need of assistance. Make sure she holds her tongue with regard to these matters. And if it is true that you must be self-controlled with regards to wine and finances (v. 8), then make sure that she too is sober. Make sure that she is self-controlled. And then finally if the male deacon is to hold the faith with a pure conscience (v. 9), then she too should be faithful in all things. She should not vol-unteer to take care of certain matters and then drop the ball. Let her be reliable in all matters.

If these things must be true of the deaconess, and more often than not, the deaconess is the wife of the deacon, then this all falls back on the deacon and the way he manages his home. That home must be managed with the right kind of faithfulness. The deacon, just like the pastor, cannot be flirtatious. He must be hopelessly devoted to his wife and remain totally faithful in act and in heart to her.

But not only must he be faithful to his wife; he must be the right kind of father to his children. He must rule his children. His children must not rule him. His children must not rule themselves. He must rule them, guide them, and lead them. In a word, he is a father, and he must act like it.

He must rule his house faithfully, rule his house fatherly, and rule his house financially. He must rule his household well. He must be properly managed, properly arranged. How can he govern the finances of a church budget when he has trouble governing the smaller budget of home? So not only must the wife and the kids be managed, but the house itself must be properly managed. It must be managed well. In a word, the deacon must not only be right in heart; he must be right in home.

The Honor of the Deacon (v. 13)

If a deacon applies all that we have said, and uses the office of a deacon well, the Bible says that he purchases to himself a good degree. And the word here translated "degree" was used of the degrees on a sundial. It refers to a step of advancement. What does this mean?

There are three primary interpretations. The first is that the deacon takes a step by being promoted to a

The Duties of a Deacon

higher office. In other words, some take this to mean that if a man is a good deacon, he has made the right step to becoming a pastor. This seems to me to be out of harmony with the context which is one of thinking of others, not self, and out of harmony with history. There have been many good deacons who have never become pastors.

The second interpretation is that the deacon makes a step of advancement in the eyes of God. It is possible that the next phrase means "boldness in approach to God." Most of the time, however, when the word *boldness* is used, it is used with reference to men.

Therefore, I think the best interpretation is that the deacon who uses his office well, purchases to himself standing in the Christian community. He gains influence among the members of the church. His faith in Christ becomes bolder because of the recognition which he has received. His faith in Christ Jesus has been found to be of impeccable variety, and the church enthusiastically endorses him.

I have pastored now for many years, and I have had all kinds of deacons. From time to time, I receive complaints about deacons. I always try to present my deacons in a positive light to my people, but some deacons give the congregation ammunition for criticism by not using the office of a deacon well. They cut their own throats. This is not necessary, for if they would use the office properly, they would rise in esteem, not diminish in it.

CHAPTER EIGHT

The Reason for Order

I Timothy 3:14-16

In II Timothy 1, we studied the message of the church. In II Timothy 2, we studied the methodology of the church. And then in II Timothy 3, we studied the men of the church. Now if the message is to be proclaimed with the proper methodology under the leadership of the proper men, there is a reason for all this. There is a reason for the order that is being suggested by the Apostle Paul.

The apostle pauses in his instructions to let Timothy know there is a reason for all this. There is a reason why these things are being written to you. Paul is not concerned merely with ecclesiastical mechanisms; he is concerned with spiritual life. These things have been given in order that people might develop and flourish spiritually.

The Apostle Would Be Absent (vv. 14-15a)

The Apostle Paul hoped to meet Timothy soon. And yet he feared that he might be delayed. Because we are talking about God's house, the church of the living God, the pillar and the ground of the truth, it is imperative that there be direction. God never intended that His church be without apostolic instruction. There is to be a continuation in apostolic doctrine (Acts 2:42). Local churches are to be characterized by continuation in the doctrine of the apostles.

65

How does this continuation occur when the apostles are absent? Paul makes the answer clear. The apostles wrote certain things. And these things which they have written unto us are meant to be our apostolic orders. Now this is important. Paul did not invest Timothy himself with apostolic authority. He did not allow his apostleship to succeed to Timothy in view of his absence. No, what took the place of Paul's person was not another person, but rather the message which Paul himself wrote. The point is clear that there is no such thing as apostolic succession. What stands today in place of the apostles is the apostolic message, the word of God.

We are told how to behave in the church of God, not by men who have taken the place of the apostles, but the message which has been penned by the apostles themselves. Therefore, it is not the church who sits in judgment on the Bible; it is the Bible which sits in judgment of the church. These things have been written to cover that period of time when the apostles are gone. These things are written to govern our behavior in the house of God. These rules of order are here to govern us in the absence of the apostles.

Our Behavior Must Be Becoming (v. 15b)

Some translations have rendered this verse "the household of God." Paul, however, is saying more than that. He is saying that we are the house of God. We are the structure in which God lives. We are the structure in which God dwells.

When Paul refers to the structure in which God

The Reason for Order

dwells, he is referring to no material building; he is referring to a spiritual assembly. God lives not in a house of wood and stone, but in bodies of flesh and bone. He lives in the assembly, in the ekklesia. The God who is in the assembly is the living God; He lives in the assembly. Dead idols are placed in temples. God, however, lives in the church.

The church is nothing less than the pillar and the ground of truth. Now be very careful about what Paul is saying and what he is not saying here. He is not giving more eminence to the church than to the truth. It is the uniform teaching of the New Testament that the church is grounded on the truth, not truth grounded on the church. What does Paul mean then when he says that the church is the ground of the truth?

The first word *pillar* helps us understand the second word *ground*. A pillar was a prop to hold something up. The word *ground* could also be used of a bulwark, and that's the sense here. The church is the custodian of the truth. This is very important when it comes to determining which version of Scripture you are going to use. One text of Scripture was produced by the natural scholarship of unregenerate men. The other text of Scripture was received by the saints as a spiritual custody. The truth is found in the body of Scripture which the church has perpetually had in custody, not in some new thing that came along in 1881. The church, not the scholar, is the holder up and protector of truth.

The church is to be digesting the truth (Revelation 10:9). The church is to be defending the truth (Philippians 1:16). The church is to be disseminating the truth (Matthew 28:18-20). The church is to be demonstrating the truth in consecrated living (Colossians 3:12-17). That's the application that Paul is making here. If God lives in the assembly and has made the church His home, causing the church to recognize the truth and be custodian of it, then we must understand that the custody of truth not only applies to having the Bible in the pew; it refers to having the Bible in life.

If it is the house of God, if it is the church of the living God, if it is the pillar and ground of truth, then we have to know how to behave ourselves as members of that place. We must conduct ourselves with the proper decorum. So Paul gave all these rules about a message of life, and a method of living, and men of leadership so that we would behave ourselves as becoming church people.

The Christ Must Be Central (v. 16)

When it comes to proper behavior, the church has commonly consented to one thing. We have debated the gap theory, the sons of God theory, and various other things. But concerning this one thing, all true believers have had no controversy. Great is the mystery of godliness. The word translated "godliness" is *eusebeia*, which refers to godly living, to the devotion of our lives to God. Christians are people who have given themselves to God. And there is no argument among Christians concerning that.

Before we were saved, we did not have a clue about

The Reason for Order

how to live. Our lives had no quality hub around which the life rotated. But that which had been previously hidden to us is now revealed. The great secret to effective living has been made manifest. As verse 16 clearly points out, the secret to effective living is none other than Jesus Christ Himself. Christ must be central. If no other doctrine is right, the doctrine of Him must be right. So let's do a brief check on our Christology.

In Christ, God became flesh (v. 16a)

There is much important doctrine here. First, Christ was eternally pre-existent. He existed prior to Bethlehem. Bethlehem for Christ was not the beginning of His existence; it was merely the moment when He assumed flesh. This is true because, second, Christ was God. The one who assumed flesh at Bethlehem was nothing less than God very God. Inferior translations may say, "He became flesh." But the most reliable manuscripts say, "God became flesh." Then third, in this statement you have the doctrine of the incarnation. God became flesh and dwelt among us. So in Christ, we have the God man; God became flesh.

To Christ, the Spirit gave witness (v. 16b)

The Holy Spirit confirmed the message of Christ. He vindicated Christ's earthly ministry. Because the glory of God was veiled in the flesh of Christ, there was a necessity for supernatural verification. The Spirit descending in the form of a dove at the baptism confirmed that Jesus was the Son of God. Because Christ was anointed by the Spirit, He was empowered to do supernatural miracles in spite of the fact that He was in a body of flesh. The Holy Spirit gave inner witness to the words of Jesus. And the Holy Spirit totally vindicated the ministry of Jesus by raising Jesus from the dead. Jesus Christ was vindicated by the Spirit. To Christ, the Spirit gave witness.

To Christ, the angels give reverence (v. 16c)

Christ was seen by angels. Angels are at the throne of God waiting to do God's bidding. If Christ was thus seen of angels, He must have been elevated to a close proximity of God's throne. Indeed, the Bible tells us that He was elevated to God's right hand, and there angels revere Him. They see Him, and He is the constant focus of their adoration and worship.

Of Christ, the world has knowledge (v. 16d)

If the Messiah has a manifestation in heaven, He also has a manifestation on earth. When Christ left His disciples, He said, "You shall be witnesses unto me." What the apostles were to teach and preach was Jesus. So they went to Jerusalem, Judea, Samaria, and the uttermost part of the earth, and the Gentiles, the heathen in darkness, began to know about Jesus. His name has circled this globe like the name of none other. He has been preached among the Gentiles. Of Christ, the world has knowledge.

The Reason for Order   71

In Christ, men have placed faith (v. 16e)

As the Messiah is preached in the world, men exercise faith in Him and so are saved. He is the object of true belief. In the world of men, the only way of salvation is through faith in the Lord Jesus Christ (Acts 4:12), and many have done just that. Christ has been believed on in the world. In Christ, men have placed their faith.

For Christ, we eagerly wait (v. 16f)

As we preach Christ among the heathen and see souls saved, we realize that this is the mandate until He returns (cf. Acts 1:8-11). Christ has been received up into glory, but we are not to stand around and look up in the sky; we have a mandate. This mandate of evangelism is being fulfilled as we await the return of Him from glory. He was received up into glory with the prospect of coming again, and for Him we eagerly wait.

So in Christ, God became flesh. To Christ, the Spirit gave witness. To Christ, the angels give reverence. Of Christ, the world must have knowledge so that in Christ, men can place faith. As they do, for Christ they will eagerly wait. I would say the Bible makes Christ central, wouldn't you?

So we need to know these principles of Christian worship because the apostles are absent; they are no longer with us. We need to know them because our behavior should be becoming those who profess Christ. We should know them because Christ must always be central, not just peripheral.

CHAPTER NINE

Errors That Plague the Church

I Timothy 4:1-5

In the previous chapter, we did a check on our Christology, and we discussed the importance of having the right doctrine, especially concerning Christ. The future behavior of the church is uniquely linked to Christ remaining central. If it is true that our future behavior is linked to proper doctrinal belief, then we have every reason to believe that Satan will try to oppose right belief. Whenever truth flourishes, error will raise its head. And so we have to be a people who not only stand for the truth, but who also recognize error and deal with it.

The Statement from the Spirit (v. la)

Whenever the Bible talks about the last days, it is talking about that economy in which we now live. Ever since the ministry of Jesus, we have been living in the last days. It is clear that Paul wrote these things to Timothy to be of a practical help to him. Therefore, even Timothy back in the first century was living in the last days.

So during the latter times, the age in which we now live, some will depart from the faith. The faith here speaks of that faith which has once for all been handed down to the saints, the Word of God. During this age we will see men apostasize. We will see men experience doctrinal departure.

Now lest we doubt this, Paul says that this is something which the Spirit speaks expressly. In other words, the Spirit is speaking in specific terms. There is nothing doubtful or vague about what the Spirit is saying. What is going to happen is being distinctly made known. Therefore, you and I should not be surprised or bewildered when it happens. We have a statement from the Spirit.

The Seduction of the Spirits (vv. 1b-2)

When we see this doctrinal departure, we need to understand where it is coming from. When people depart from the faith, we need to understand what is behind this departure. Men depart from the faith because they have given heed to seducing spirits. So, there is not only the Spirit of truth which speaks explicitly, but there are also spirits of error who speak seductively.

The doctrinal error which these people have embraced is nothing less than the doctrines of demons. Do you know that the devil has a doctrinal statement? It is a doctrinal statement of error, a statement which has enticed people away from the truth of God's Word.

So whenever we see men who are speaking doctrinal lies, when we see men who purport to be agents of God but are mere hypocrites, we know exactly where that came from. It came from the seducing influence of demonic spirits. This heresy is nothing less than the doctrines of demons.

These men who are hypocritical liars are men who have had their consciences seared. Two things are involved in searing. When a farmer sears or brands an animal, he does so in order to show that the animal belongs

Errors That Plague the Church

to him. So when we see hypocritical liars whose consciences are seared, we know they belong to the devil. They have branded themselves as belonging to him.

Second, when something is branded or cauterized, the nerve endings are deadened. That area which has been cauterized is past feeling (cf. Ephesians 4:19). So, these people are past feeling; their consciences are no longer sensitive to the Word of God. They have been duped by seducing spirits. Their doctrine is demonic. These hypocritical liars are not sensitive to the Word of God and thus they reveal themselves to belong to Satan. They have been seduced by the spirits.

The Substance of the Sect (v. 3)

Now up to this point, we have been given some strong words. The Spirit is expressing Himself about people who will be seduced spiritually, and we are on the edge of our seats to know what this serious doctrinal error is. When we read verse 3, we are almost shocked that this is it. This is what the Spirit is so expressive about? This is the great doctrinal error? Yes, this is it.

Men are going to prohibit two things. They are going to prohibit marriage, and they are going to prohibit the eating of certain foods. Now at first this does not seem like too big a deal. Why are men who prohibit marriage and prohibit the eating of certain foods seduced men who have swallowed the doctrine of demons? Why are these men hypocritical liars? The answer is given in the latter part of verse 3. They are such because their admonitions contain a dangerous implication.

God has given man many good things to enjoy. To a man, the two greatest sensual pleasures that God has given for his enjoyment are sex and food. Mankind derives no greater sensual pleasure than he does through the sex act and through eating. There is nothing wrong with this provided they are done properly. God created these things for us to receive. We ought to receive them thankfully. We ought to be thankful that God gave us marriage to enjoy the sex act. We ought to be thankful that God gave us food to enjoy. These pleasurable experiences have been created by God for us, and we should receive them with thanksgiving.

The Christian community sometimes gets this all muddled. They want to place these sensual things as only pertaining to the lost. Sex is not just for unbelievers; sex in marriage is for believers (Hebrews 13:14). Marriage is honorable in all, that is, among all people. The Catholic Church says that certain devout Christians should not marry. That's not what God says. God says that He created marriage for those who believe and know the truth.

The Catholic Church would also say that on certain days you ought to abstain from certain foods. This would prove your devotion to God. Paul says, however, that food was created for the enjoyment of those who believe and know the truth. Even today evangelical dieticians are talking about the world's diet verses the believer's diet. The diet of the believer is more exclusive than the diet of the worldling. This is nothing more than Protestant Lent. Those who know and believe the truth are to enjoy food just as much as the lost.

What makes these prohibitions so satanic is that they strike at the very nature of God. These prohibitions imply that God does not want believers to have fun. They portray God as one who sits up in Heaven and delights in taking away enjoyable things from His creatures. This whole concept paints God as one who is to be feared if I do not live monastically. Nothing could be further from the truth. God wants you to enjoy life, and this includes sex and food. Therefore, receive what God has created for you with thanksgiving.

The Sentiment of the Saint (vv. 4-5)

Now if God is not a cosmic kill-joy, but God actually wants us to have sex and food, then what should our attitude be? First, we must understand that God is a good Creator. Therefore, whatever God made must be good. If God created the sex and the food, then they must be good, for they came from God (James 1:17). Where did sex come from? Where did food come from? They both came from God. Therefore, they must be good.

Now if they came from God and are therefore good things, we must not refuse them. And the word translated "refused" literally means "to throw away." The word is used metaphorically of counting something as taboo. In all kinds of heathen cults, certain foods are considered taboo. The intelligent Christian is not to be sucked into this way of thinking. He is to receive these items with thanksgiving.

Don't let people put you on a guilt trip for being married or for eating certain foods. You receive it and be thankful for it. Now, of course, this implies that we say grace before we eat. We are to pray before we eat, and many times that prayer will contain quotes of the Scripture. These moments of grace actually sanctify the food, that is, they set the food apart for a sacred purpose. The sacred purpose is that of nourishing the Christian body to do the work of the Lord. So food and sex, far from being evil in purpose, can actually accomplish a holy purpose if we recognize God's benevolence and thank Him for it.

In Corinth, what brought sickness to the person, was not the physical composition of the food. Everybody at Corinth ate from the same bread and drank from the same cup. The disease occurred, not because of what was being eaten, but because of the spiritual condition of the one who was eating it (I Corinthians 11:28-30). Many today are concentrating so much on the physical taboos of diet, but are giving no consideration to the state of their soul. What is most important is the attitude, or the sentiment of the saint. He must receive the food with thanksgiving.

CHAPTER TEN

Methods of Dealing with False Teachers

I Timothy 4:6-16

Last chapter, we looked at the fact that false teaching is going to raise its ugly head. Some are going to depart from the faith giving heed to seducing spirits. When these doctrinal departures occur, how is the pastor to deal with it? What are the methods of dealing with false teachers? This is what Paul is discussing in the passage before us currently.

The Mandate to Follow (v. 6)

The Apostle Paul now begins a personal directive to Timothy, but this statement is meant to serve all ministers of the Gospel who have to deal with doctrinal error. We are to put the brethren in remembrance of these things. In other words, we need to warn people about the doctrinal errors that are out there. The verb translated "put in remembrance" means much more than to suggest; the Greeks used the word of giving commands. The word literally means "to place under." Because false doctrine exists, Christians need to be placed under certain directives.

Ministers prove themselves to be good ministers of Jesus Christ when they do this. There is much erroneous doctrine out there. Because there is erroneous doctrine, we need to give our people a healthy alternative. A pastor who does not give his people a healthy alternative is

79

not worthy to be a minister. We need to be continually nourishing our people up in the words of the faith. We need to give our people a steady continual diet of the body of Christian doctrine. There is no better means of spiritual nourishment other than dwelling on the great truths of the faith. The false teachers in verse 3 were all worried about man's physical diet; Paul says the good preacher is concerned about people's spiritual diet.

Good doctrine is what we are hoping to attain. This is the standard which we are to follow. If we do not want our people to follow false doctrine, doctrines of demons, then we must constantly place before them good doctrine as the standard. The best refutation of error is a positive presentation of the truth. And this is the mandate which the preacher is to follow.

The Method of Fulfillment (vv. 7-10)

If we are going to constantly place good doctrine before our people as the standard, then this means we are going to refuse that which is profane. The word translated "profane" comes from a root which means to go, and hence the word came to refer to that which may be walked on. Some teachings that exist out there are not worthy of elevation; they should be trampled. Those types of doctrines we should avoid, for they are nothing more than old wives' fables. The word translated "fables" comes from the word *muthoi*, from which we get our word *myths*. These myths are called old wives' myths, indicating their frivolous character. There can be no compromise with this stuff, no toleration. Such

Methods of Dealing with False Teachers 81

teaching must be refused, and the word that Paul uses suggests a strong refusal.

In order to help us refuse this junk, we have to replace it with something positive. To help us understand this principle, Paul turns to athletics. Instead of being concerned with stuff that characterizes old women, we need to act like strong robust men. But Paul here is not talking about being robust externally; he is talking about being robust internally. The false teachers are all concerned about the body, but Paul wants to go deeper than that. Bodily exercise may be profitable for some things, but godliness is profitable in all things.

Bodily exercise, whatever benefit it may have, is a benefit only for this life. After death, whatever we achieved through bodily exercise will no longer be applicable. But godliness not only profits for the life that now is; godliness also profits for the life which is to come. God wants a Christian to have the best of both worlds, this world and the next, and the way the best of both worlds is achieved is through godliness.

This is a faithful saying; this is a true word. The statement that godliness is profitable for all things is a statement on which you can go to the bank. It is a statement which is worthy of your acceptation and application.

That being the case, therefore, we labor. The word *labor* is used of strenuous activity to the point of sweat and fatigue. Paul uses the word *labor* as a synonym with running (Philippians 2:16). Hence the word *labor* was frequently used of athletic fatigue, and in the context, that is the sense here. Because godliness is profitable for all things, it demands every ounce of energy that a man possesses.

When a man becomes conscious and becomes constantly devoted to the training of his body, many times people will laugh at his devotion. They will ridicule the life of self-denial that the athlete has embraced. If that is true in the physical realm, how much more is it true in the spiritual realm? When you begin to exercise yourself strenuously in godliness, you will suffer reproach.

But the athlete continues despite the ridicule because he has a goal that he wants to achieve. Now if an athlete can endure the ridicule, because of the hope of success, how much more should you and I be willing to endure the reproach of this world? We have a hope that is much greater than that of the athlete. We have a hope that is rooted and fixed in the living God. The preservation of life is not ultimately rooted in physical exercise; it is rooted in God who is the source of life. Physical exercise is not the ultimate savior; God is.

This applies not only to physical life, but more importantly to spiritual life. God preserves all men, but especially those who believe. Those who have placed their faith in the living God are preserved like no others are preserved. Because God is our Savior, we whole-heartedly give ourselves to Him like we give ourselves to no other person and like we give ourselves to no other thing. The mandate we have been given to follow is methodically fulfilled by a strenuous devotion to godliness.

The Mindset of Fearlessness (vv. 11-16)

The things that Paul has been saying about godliness need to be addressed. They need to be taught, but not merely taught; they need to be commanded. In other words, they need to be taught with firmness. As we already discussed in chapter 1, Timothy was a fearful person who was prone to timidity. And part of this timidity was due to Timothy's youth.

Many of the Ephesian Christians would have been older than their pastor. It was not inconceivable that some of them would have looked down on him with disfavor and contempt because he was younger. But there was a way that Timothy could counter-balance this contempt. He could live in an exemplary manner.

There are certain characteristics which come naturally to those who are young. Sometimes they are not serious. Sometimes they are not prudent. Sometimes they are not considerate of others. Sometimes they are not trustworthy. Sometimes they do not exercise control over their passions. Timothy needs to do his best to excel in these very areas, and by doing so, he will silence his critics.

By so living, Timothy will prove to those in the church that authority is not contingent upon age; it is contingent upon character. Every young pastor should give heed to this six-fold requirement. The first two things mentioned (word and conversation) refer to Timothy's public life, but the remaining four (charity, spirit, faithfulness, and purity) refer to Timothy's inner soul. What we are in our soul reflects in our behavior.

So if Timothy is right in his heart, and that is manifested in his actions, criticisms will wane and people will heed what Timothy has to say. When Timothy stands behind the pulpit to speak to the people, he needs to give attention to three things. First, he needs to give attention to reading. In the synagogue, worship always included the reading of the Word of God. And the church continued that practice.

Once the Word of God was read, there ought to be public exhortation based on that text. The Word of God is not merely to be read; it is to be used to encourage and motivate the people to a specific way of living. But at the same time that exhortation must give attention to doctrine, to the great truths of the Christian faith. So Timothy must read the Word of God and then use that reading to encourage the people to live right and believe right.

This was the entire reason why Timothy was ordained. God had given him the office, that privilege, that gift for the purpose of doing exactly what was stated in verse 13. Therefore, don't neglect doing what you were ordained to do. At ordinations, there is usually a charge to the candidate which stresses the obligations of the pastor. That prophecy or charge is not to be neglected. The other elders gathered around and placed their hands on that man's head devoting him to that specific task. Don't let their actions go to waste. Fulfill your ministry. Those pastors publicly endorsed you. Don't neglect that gift of being a pastor by failing to fulfill your obligations.

Methods of Dealing with False Teachers 85

Now in order to fulfill our obligations, we must meditate consistently on what is required of us. Keep the job of the pastorate constantly on your mind. Ruminate on your obligations; constantly think about them; let them be at the forefront of your thinking.

But just don't think about it. Give yourself to it. Teenagers say sometimes, "He's really into it", and they will name some particular activity. He's really into basketball. He's really into soccer. Well, a pastor really needs to be into pastoring. He needs to be totally absorbed with it. He ought to be completely immersed in it. You can't get bogged down in civilian affairs, if God has called you to be a soldier (II Timothy 2:4). You must give yourself wholly to it.

Make no bones about it, preacher; people are watching you. The preacher is constantly under public observation. What ultimately we should desire to impress the Christian community with is not our brilliant exposition, or our attractive personality, but with our true Christian development. Our spiritual prosperity, our surplus of character; that is what should appear to all.

So preacher, take heed to yourself. It is not only mandatory to keep a watchful eye over the flock; you must also keep a watchful eye over yourself, for you are not only a shepherd; you are also a sheep. Therefore, always keep your eye on yourself, both on how you behave and on what you teach. Continue to live right and speak right.

Paul said in Philippians 2:12 that we need to work out our own salvation. And if that is true of anyone, it is true of the preacher. If he is the director of spiritual development, then he must certainly direct his own spiritual development. To be sure we want others to work out their own salvation, but they will only do it if they see us modeling it. People are to follow us because we follow Christ. And that demands no spirit of timidity; it demands courage: courage to do it ourselves and courage to demand it of others.

CHAPTER ELEVEN

Dealing with Widows

I Timothy 5:1-16

Within any age church, there are varying age groups. We have older men and younger men. We have older women and younger women. Sometimes the pastor is perplexed as to how to deal with one or more of these classes. Sometimes the way old men behave, there is a tendency to rebuke them. The word translated "rebuke" here is a strong word; it means to censure severely. If a man is advanced in years, he should be spared that kind of treatment. This is not to say that correction is never necessary, but when it is necessary, entreat that man as if he were your father. The same is true of older women; they should be treated as if they were your mother.

Now towards the younger members of the congregation, there can be more of a fraternal spirit. Younger men can be viewed as brothers. Younger women can be viewed as sisters. There can be more of an equal footing with them. But don't become too chummy with the younger women. Whatever relationship you have with them, make sure it is one of purity. Make sure that the younger women of the congregation are handled just like sisters.

The point that is being given in these opening verses is that there is a respect that is due old age. The church in general, and the pastor in specific, should have a heart for the elderly of the congregation. Specifically, this is

87

true of widows. What should the church's attitude be toward those who have lost their husbands?

The Widows Who Are in Need (v. 1-8)

Paul tells us that we are to treat older women, especially widows, like mothers, and we do this by honoring them. Remember the Bible says, "Honor thy father and thy mother." Therefore, if the older widow is to be treated like a mother, she should be honored. Now to be sure, the word *honor* carries with it the idea of respect, but it also carries with it the idea of material support, hence the word *honorarium*. Clearly, Jesus viewed the honoring of parents to include financial support (Matthew 15:4-5). And as we will see in this context, we can honor widows by helping them financially.

We should not look down on certain individuals just because they are poor; the Bible says just the opposite. These people are worthy of our honor. Now, of course, God does not want us to give away the church money to any and all widows, regardless of whether they need the money or not. No, the money should be given to those who are widows indeed, that is, widows genuinely destitute. If there are widows in the church, and they are really in need, it is our responsibility to care for them.

Now obviously, if we are going to financially care for widows, there must be some guidelines. And so Paul lays them down for us here. The word here translated "nephews" is a general word for descendants, and usually it refers to grand-children and great grand-children. In other words, if the widow has children and/or grand-

Dealing with Widows

children, these are to help her first. They are to requite their parents before the church ever does. Piety, before it is ever shown on the church level, must be shown on the home level.

Certainly in light of the commandment, "Honor your father and mother", this is an action that is acceptable with God. So, first the priority comes to the children before it ever comes to the church. So the first requirement for supporting a widow is that she must be desolate, that is, she must be entirely alone with no family members to take care of her.

The second thing that must be true of a widow before she can be supported by the church is that she must be one who trusts in God. In other words, the widows who are helped by the church are widows that are believers. They have a hope that is fixed in the direction of God. The church is not obligated to help any and all destitute widows, but only those who are among the Christian community.

Then third, we get even more narrow, and Paul says the widow must not only be a believer; she must be a woman of constant prayer. Of course, all of this reminds us of Anna. Anna was a woman who lived right on the temple compound; she was supported by the church, if you will. Anna was qualified for that support because she gave herself to prayer (Luke 2:37). Now some widows are capable of work; we will see that later on. But some widows are not capable of work. Nevertheless, these widows can do something to reimburse the church: they can pray. This is a work that they can continue in and should continue in night and day if they desire support.

Many times when a woman loses her husband, she is tempted to support herself by immoral living. If she gives herself sexually to another man, he will take care of her. If a woman engages in this kind of activity, she is not to be supported, for she reveals that she has no spiritual life in her. Even though she is physically alive, she is spiritually dead. As such, she has no claim on the church's support.

And so here we have the commands by which the church is to abide if it wants to remain blameless in the support of widows. Widows must be spiritually fit, and they must have no remaining relatives. Paul sensed that the item here that really needed to be stressed was the one of younger people taking care of their parents. We are to provide for our own within the church, but this is especially true of those who are in our own family. To deny this responsibility is to deny the essence of Christian faith which is loving God and loving your fellow man. To not provide for your family is to live worse than an infidel. Even infidels acknowledge the responsibility of providing for their families. It is unthinkable that Christian people would lag behind the pagan standards of the world. We must take care of the widows who are in need.

The Widows Who Can Work (vv 9-10)

Now obviously, all widows are to be helped in specific instances where they are in distress. But what about

Dealing with Widows

widows who needed systematic help? There were certain widows who need on-going financial care. What should the church do about these? Well, the church had a number of widows that it supported on a regular basis. But there were requirements for being counted in that number.

First, the widow had to be at least sixty years of age. And we will discuss a little bit later why this is an important requirement. Second, the widow must be the wife of one man. In other words, if the widow gets remarried after the death of her husband, she should not assume that the church will take care of her; that is the responsibility of her new husband. The third thing that should be true of this woman is that her life should have been characterized by good works.

I believe the pecking order here is significant. The first and most important work of a woman is to bring up children. Nothing else takes the place of child-care in the life of the lady. A mother makes no greater contribution to her home than the contribution of raising godly children. Many women, rather than raising their children, let the day care raise their children because they feel their most important obligation to the home is financial. It is not. The most important contribution a woman can make is the raising of her children.

Her second obligation is hospitality. But notice even the ministry is not outside the home; it is inviting people into the home. When travelers come in, she lodges them and washes their feet. Then only after those things have been done does she expand to general sympathy and benevolent ministry. These are the good works that she should have generally followed if she wants systematic support.

Of course, such widows would be of inestimable value in caring for orphans, entertaining visiting Christians, and attending to many of the menial tasks that need to be done around the church. Therefore, before we take a widow on in a systematic way, it would be prudent to make sure that there is something that she can do for the church to earn that money. Whether such is true in each specific case can be determined by looking at the way the woman behaved herself in her younger days. She should be a woman who is not afraid of hard work.

The Widows Who Are Young (vv. 11-16)

Now as we stated earlier, only women who were at least sixty years of age could be supported systematically by the church. Now we see why those who were younger were refused. Obviously, these younger widows could be helped in specific instances when they were in distress, but they were not to be helped systematically. The reason that this is true is because these women had a strong likelihood of remarriage.

The word here translated "wax wanton" is only found here in the New Testament, but it is used in secular Greek of an ox trying to escape from underneath a yoke. If the opportunity for marriage came along, these younger women would try to get out of their church responsibilities. They would not want to be tied to their

Dealing with Widows

church duties. This chafing against church responsibility is nothing less than a chafing against Christ Himself. Christ has so bound Himself to His church that fighting against the church is fighting against Christ. So here is this woman who has pledged herself in service to the church and now she wants to renege on that vow in order to get married.

Such a violation of commitment is fighting against Christ, and it will receive nothing but judgment. Such actions are a casting aside of the first faith, that is, casting off what they first pledged themselves to. They have vowed a vow, and now they are deferring to pay it because they want to get married.

Now when that happens, when a woman who is on the church register of widows gets interested in a man, she is not going to fulfill her church obligations zealously. Rather, just the opposite is true; she will learn to be idle. The fact that Paul uses the term *learn* reveals that this is no unconscious decision. This woman is deliberately becoming slack in her obligations.

This produces two things. She will wander from house to house. She will misuse her opportunities in visitation, and rather than ministering, she will be merely socializing. The inevitable result of that will be that she will become a tale-bearer and a busy-body. Rather than being engaged in ministry, speaking words of encouragement, she will be characterized by idle gossip, speaking things about which she should have kept her mouth closed.

The way to avoid all this is for the younger women

to marry, to bear children, and to raise those children for the Lord. Rather than just lazily telling stories in other houses, these women need to get married, bear children, and manage their own homes rather than trying to manage everybody else's.

The whole purpose for this is that we do not want the adversary to speak reproachfully. The devil is a slanderer, and when women slander fellow Christians from house to house, they play right into the devil's hands. The word translated "occasion" is a military term which refers to a base of operations. Such women should not be the base from which the devil operates. Lest we think this will not happen, Paul says some have already done it. They have turned aside from active ministry and are engaged in slandering others. They are following right in the devil's footsteps.

So, if there is any way possible that we can help these widows until they marry, let's do it. Let's do it so the church will be relieved of this responsibility and will be better prepared to help those widows who are really destitute.

CHAPTER TWELVE

Honoring Your Pastors

I Timothy 5:17-25

If it is true that honor is due to widows, it is also true that honor is due to elders. The word translated "elder" is the Greek term *presbuteros*, which can refer to an old man, and the word is used this way in 5:1. But the word *elder* can also refer to an official in the church. Paul, for example, left Timothy in Crete to ordain elders (Titus 1:5-7), and in describing the qualifications for being an elder, Paul says, "A bishop must be blameless." Obviously, in this context, the word *elder* and the word *bishop* are used interchangeably. Similarly, Peter says that elders are to feed the flock of God (I Peter 5:1-2). The word translated "feed" in this text is the same word translated "pastor" in Ephesians 4:11. Elders are people who pastor the flock of God. In Acts 20:17, Paul addresses the Ephesian elders. And to these Ephesian elders Paul says, "The Holy Ghost has made you overseers (the same word translated "bishop" elsewhere) to feed (the same word translated "pastor" elsewhere) the flock of God." Elders are bishops who pastor.

Obviously, the New Testament uses the term *bishop*, the term *elder*, and the term *pastor* to describe the same office. The term *elder* describes the nature of the man; he is mature in the faith. The term *bishop* describes the function of the man; he oversees. The term *pastor* describes the motive of the man; he oversees with loving

95

concern. When Paul uses the term *elder* in I Timothy 5:17, he is using it in that technical sense of a church official. He is talking about a bishop, a pastor. Paul says that pastors ought to be honored. How is this to be done?

Honor Them with Compensation (vv. 17-18)

The New Testament pattern is always for a church to have a plurality of pastors. But within that plurality, there should be a presiding elder, what we would call today a senior pastor. For example, Acts 21:18 clearly indicates that there was a plurality of pastors at the church in Jerusalem, but James was the presiding elder, the senior pastor. This is clearly evident when you read the account of the Jerusalem Council in Acts 15.

So all elders rule, but there are some who rule exceptionally well. And these are the ones who labor in the word and doctrine. For example, a large church may have numerous pastors. They may have an associate pastor, a youth pastor, a children's pastor, a bus pastor, and an education pastor. But over all these pastors is one pastor who rules well, and his rule is characterized as labor in the word and doctrine. He has the vast majority of the pulpit time. He is the primary teacher of that church. All elders are to be honored. But that presiding elder, that senior pastor, is especially to be honored.

Part of that honor includes honorarium, and to prove this point, Paul quotes Deuteronomy 25:4. When oxen were treading corn, they were not to be muzzled. They were allowed to eat from the corn that they were

Honoring Your Pastors

treading. And in so doing, the oxen were paid for the work that they were doing. Paul, both here and in I Corinthians, makes the point that this is applicable to the payment of ministers (I Corinthians 9:9-11). The passage in the law is given not just as a rule for animals, but as a principle that people who work should be paid. Thus, the minister who labors in the word should be financially compensated. If he ministers to the church's spiritual needs, the church should minister to his material needs.

Jesus says essentially the same thing in Luke 10:7. The laborer is worthy of his reward. Paul uses these two Scriptures to admonish Timothy about the financial package for pastors. Too often a stingy attitude has been maintained by God's people in compensating their pastors financially when those pastors have faithfully ministered God's Word. Now certainly the pastor himself should not be characterized as moneygrubbing. Paul has already talked about that in 3:3, but the congregation's attitude should be one of ample provision. Pastors who devote ample time and energy to study should be financially compensated. Elders should be honored with compensation.

Honor Their Reputation (vv. 19-21)

The word here translated "before" carries with it the idea of "upon." The idea is that an accusation against a pastor must be based upon the oral testimony of two or three witnesses, and if it is not based upon the testimony of two or three witnesses, the accusation is not to be even taken up or entertained. The point is that a pastor is to be carefully protected against malicious intent.

Now that is not to say that a pastor is never in the wrong. There will be times when an accusation should be taken up and entertained, and sometimes that accusation will be sustained by the facts. If indeed the pastor is wrong, then he should be rebuked, and Paul goes so far as to say that he should be rebuked in the presence of the entire congregation. Such public rebuke will have an effect upon the congregation. They will fear the consequences of sin. Such public rebuke will result in church-wide purity. There is a balance here. The pastor's reputation is to be carefully protected, but if he has tarnished it himself, then there needs to be public censure.

Now the key thing that will help us in this regard is a lack of partiality. Partiality hurts in this matter both ways. When people are prejudiced against a pastor, they bring accusations that are not true. When people are prejudiced in favor of the pastor, they ignore accusations that are true. So always in this matter the personality of the pastor has nothing to do with it. Our pastoral preference has nothing at all to do with the issue at hand. This is a situation where nothing should be done with partiality.

This is very solemn. Notice the serious language here. "I charge thee before God, and the Lord Jesus Christ, and the elect angels." In other words, the world is not the only one watching the way the church conducts itself in these matters. All of heaven is watching too, and the reference to the elect angels may bring a

Honoring Your Pastors   99

hint of eschatology into this charge. In light of the fact
that heaven is watching, and in light of the fact that God
is coming in the person of Christ with His holy angels,
we need to handle church disciplinary matters right, especially when they are done against the pastorate. We
need to honor the reputation of our pastors.

Honor Their Installation (vv. 22-25)

Now in light of what has just been said about discipline, we may be tempted to think that laying hands
on a pastor here speaks of jacking his jaw. But the laying on of hands was a technical phrase that was used of
ordaining a man to public ministry. Ordination should
only take place after thorough investigation. Part of the
reason why ministers have to be disciplined is that they
were placed into the pastorate too early. And the church
has to bear some of the responsibility for this.

When we place a man prematurely into the office,
and then that man fails, we are a partaker of that man's
sins. We are co-responsible for wrongs which he subse-
quently commits. We should not place novices in that
position to begin with. Timothy should make sure that
he appoints only pure men, keeping himself pure in the
process.

Paul had no doubts as to Timothy being conscien-
tious. Timothy had formed the habit of drinking nothing but water as a matter of conscience. However, in the
east, water is far from safe. If one insists on drinking
nothing but water, dysentery may result. Consequently,
in order to help Timothy overcome his stomach trouble

and related ailments, which appear to be coming upon him thick and fast, Timothy is told to drink some wine.

I would make several observations here. John R. Rice was of the opinion that the wine here was merely grape juice. There are several reasons why I disagree. First, when a person is sick, the doctor tells him to drink plenty of juice. The fact that Paul limits the wine to a little bit implies it was alcoholic. Second, if unfermented wine is under discussion, how would this be a matter of conscience? I have never heard of anyone having a conviction against grape juice. The very fact that Paul addresses it here as a matter of conscience reveals that alcoholic wine is under discussion, and Paul tells Timothy to drink some wine, not much wine, but a little wine.

And clearly the use of the wine here is medicinal. It is for Timothy's infirmities. As Wuest aptly observes, Paul is speaking here of wine as a medicine, not as a beverage. Just like drugs should be taken for health reasons, not for reason of enjoyment, so alcohol should be taken. It is a drug which was intended for medicinal purposes, not recreational purposes. Even today certain medicines contain alcohol. And that is the intended purpose of alcohol.

Timothy is right to want to have a proper testimony and keep himself pure, but taking alcohol as medicine is no compromise of that purity. Timothy's attention with regard to purity should be focused on who is being recommended to the gospel ministry.

The point here is that those who are recommended to the ministry should be observed for a protracted pe-

Honoring Your Pastors

riod of time. Hasty action is based on first impressions, and first impressions many times are wrong. Some men's sins are clearly evident. There is no scrutiny even necessary; the first time you meet them you would judge them unfit for spiritual office. The very thought of nominating such a man is preposterous, but other people's sins are more hidden. These sins don't reveal themselves until you have known the person for a while. Therefore, if you quickly install a man as a pastor, you might choose an unworthy candidate. You might have chosen a person whose culpability lies deeper than the surface.

The reverse of that is true as well. There are some worthy men, whose actions are not in the limelight, who are easily overlooked. When you act hastily, not only do you choose incompetent men, but you also overlook qualified men. The whole situation demands extreme caution.

In the final analysis, this protects the honor and dignity of the pastoral office. The reason that so many people treat the pastorate with contempt and a lack of respect is because we have allowed contemptible and disrespectable men to hold the office. We need to restore honor and dignity to the office making sure that it is held by only qualified men.

CHAPTER THIRTEEN

Slaves and Masters

I Timothy 6:1-2

The Roman world was full of slaves. It has been estimated that in Rome itself at one time a third of the inhabitants were slaves. Now obviously, in churches where the membership included numerous slaves, the relationship between these slaves and their masters was a pressing problem. Slaves enjoyed equality of status within the church, but a decided social inferiority in their respective households. Of course, this was an irreconcilable antithesis which found its only solution in the abolition of slavery, but in Paul's day it was impossible for this deeply-rooted system to be completely overturned. Therefore, Paul gave interim Christian rules to help in the relationship that existed between slaves and masters.

There were two specific scenarios which needed to be addressed. Some slaves who were Christians belonged to masters who were unbelievers. This situation is addressed in verse 1. There were also some believing slaves who had masters who were Christians. This situation is addressed in verse 2. In each situation, there is a particular danger that Paul is trying to avoid.

Slaves Who Have Christless Masters (v. 1)

It is clear from Paul's choice of words that we are not talking here about merely servants, that is, hired hands.

103

The word here translated "servants" is *douloi,* which means "bond-slaves." This is made clear by the fact that Paul says these slaves are under the yoke. The power of the master over the slave was absolute. The slave was counted as nothing more than a service animal.

Indeed, this was permissible according to Roman law. Masters were legally allowed to treat their slaves harshly. They could be condemned to hard labor, chained, severely lashed, and branded. The master could even legally crucify his own slave if he wanted to. The very fact that Paul says these slaves are "under the yoke" reveals that non-Christian owners viewed their slaves as little more than cattle. The phrase brings into vivid view servile social conditions that existed at that time.

Here is a Christian slave. He has found liberty in the Lord Jesus Christ. He understands that in Christ Jesus there is no respecter of persons. This slave obviously would begin to think to himself, "How can my master treat me like this? If in the eyes of God there is no respect of persons, how can my master treat me in this harsh and tyrannical way?" It is interesting that the word Paul uses for "master" is not the usual word for master. Paul does not use the normal word *kurios* which is normally translated "lord." Instead, he uses the word for "despot" which stresses the absolute authority of the slave-owner. Here is a man who wields absolute authority over a slave just as a farmer wields absolute authority over a service animal, but Paul says that in spite of the fact that your master has placed you under the yoke, count him worthy of all honor.

Slaves and Masters 105

As hard a lesson as it is for us to learn, there is something more important than the way we are personally treated. What is more important is the name of God and the doctrine of God. It is one thing for us to be treated poorly; it is quite another thing for the cause of Christ to suffer reproach.

God's name speaks of God's character, God's person. God's doctrine speaks of the Word of God. The teaching of the Gospel would become contemptible in the eyes of these masters if their Christian slaves treated them with disdain and rebellion. There is something more important than our personal feelings, and it is the name of God and the doctrine of God. These must not be exposed to ridicule or abuse. Therefore, I must be willing to take abuse so that God's cause is not abused.

Slaves Who Have Christian Masters (v. 2)

If a slave who had an unbelieving master was tempted to view that master with contempt, the slave who had a believing master was tempted to shirk his responsibilities. The slave who had a believing master might say, "If my master is really a Christian, how can he keep me as his slave? His faith doesn't amount to much. Besides, how can I be equal to my master in the church, and yet inferior to him at home?" In the church there was neither bond nor free (Galatians 3:28), but at home it was a different story. Obviously, this would lead to trouble.

One thing that a slave is forgetting in this scenario is that he is in a privileged position. If the Christian master sold him to an unbelieving household, it would not make the situation better; it would make it worse for the slave. When a slave was in the household of a believer, the discipline and the required service were less taxing. This master's ownership had been tempered by the love of Christ. These masters began to see their slaves, not as cattle, but as brothers. Therefore, a slave in this kind of environment should not be despised by his master. Rather, he should recognize that he is in an enviable position over other slaves, and because he is in an exceptionally privileged position, he should render exceptional service.

Now the last phrases in verse 2 are somewhat ambiguous, not in what they say, but with regard to whom they apply. Some commentators believe that the phrases apply to the masters. Because the masters are faithful and loving masters, they should reap the benefit of adequate service. Other commentators believe the phrase applies to the slaves. Slaves should be loving and faithful in their service because they have reaped the benefit of having a believing master. Perhaps, however, Paul was purposefully ambiguous. Perhaps Paul wants to remind both masters and slaves that they should be faithful and beloved, and in so doing they will both partake of benefit. There is a mutual affection that is to exist between the two.

These things are to be taught and exhorted. The present tense here implies continuous action. Keep on teaching these things. Keep on exhorting these things. What Paul has been saying with regards to slaves and their masters must be constantly in the ears of the

Slaves and Masters

people. Timothy must teach these things and get them into the minds of the people, but not just their minds. It must get into their wills as well. So he must not only teach it; he must urge that these things be done.

The point is, contrary to public opinion, propositions concerning the faith are not subjective and relative. We do not arrive at truth by asking our brother, "What do you think? What is your opinion?" Paul has accepted certain facts about daily living as the truth of God. Because it is the truth of God, he wants it to be taught. He wants Timothy to urge people to accept these principles and apply them to their daily lives.

Especially when we are talking about submission to authority that is froward, our flesh naturally rebels against such a thought. It is not a matter of whether that authority is at home, at church, or at work. We naturally rebel against mean bosses. But the fact of the matter is that submission to those who are harsh, distinctively brands us as Christians. There is nothing more Christ-like than when a person is reviled to revile not again. Now this is something which our flesh does not like to hear, but it is something which Paul says must be taught and urged upon the congregation.

CHAPTER FOURTEEN

The Errors of False Teaching

I Timothy 6:3-5

At the end of verse 2, Paul told Timothy to teach and exhort certain things. The reason why the truth of God needs to be taught and exhorted is that some men will teach otherwise. The Christian pastor must always be careful to delineate the truth because false teachers will be careful to delineate error. Error is something concerning which we must always be on guard because error always results in contamination. This passages tells us three things about error.

Error Is Unhealthy (vv. 3-4a)

The word here translated "consent" literally means "to approach", and the word came to be used in Greek of approaching something and joining oneself to it. The true teacher is to adhere to healthy words. He is not merely to agree with them. He is to come over and join himself to them. He is not only to agree; he is to express that agreement. He is to chime in to healthy words.

Healthy or wholesome words are the words of our Lord Jesus Christ. This does not merely mean words which were spoken by Jesus, though that is involved. It refers to words about Jesus, that is, Christian truth. We are not to be sucked into false teaching, especially regarding Christ, for such teaching is not in our spiritual best interest. What is in our spiritual best interest is the

109

truth about Christ, for this truth, and this truth alone, results in godliness. As we will see down in verses 4 and 5, false teaching results in ungodliness.

In other words, to be sucked into false doctrine is to be spiritually unhealthy. False teachers are characterized by pride. They live in a system which has been developed by man, not God. They live in a mental, moral, and spiritual world of their own making and having done so, they are completely out of touch with reality. They are not dealing with things the way they are. They are dealing with things the way they want them to be and that is nothing short of pride. It is to say that man's way is better than God's way.

When a person because of pride rejects the healthy content of Scripture, and fails to function according to reality, he becomes sick. The word here translated "doting" is the Greek term *noseo*, from which we get our word *nausea*. It literally means "to be sick." When people reject the healthy teaching of God's Word, they become spiritually sick.

He would rather argue than be well. There are some people who would rather fight with the doctor than take the medicine, and that's the way false teachers are with God and man. They would rather argue than take the medicine for their spiritual ailment. They have a morbid craving for argumentation, and being in that state, they stay spiritually sick. Error is unhealthy.

Error Is Ungodly (vv. 4b-5a)

Now when a person takes a delight in unhealthy

The Errors of False Teaching

quibbling, it will bear bitter fruits. All the results mentioned are mental activities which are listed with a discernible progression. A person who wants to stay spiritually unhealthy will become progressively ungodly. If it is likened to a disease, it will spread. Error will result in ever-increasing ungodliness.

The first thing that he mentions is envy. When people become engaged in word battles, they become filled with malignant ill will towards one another. They will be filled with poisonous spite because they are envious of coming out on top.

Envy leads to strife. The word *strife* is found four times in the New Testament, and each time the word is linked with envy. When people have bitter ill will towards one another, they are unwilling to admit defeat. Bitter discord follows, and the men begin to constantly contradict one another. There is strife.

Strife leads to railings. The underlying Greek term is the word normally translated "blasphemies", and it refers to abusive speech. Sometimes it refers to abusive speech against God, and sometimes, as is the case here, it refers to abusive speech against our fellow man. Scornful and insolent language becomes directed against each other in the form of defamation and slander. Men begin to rail on one another.

That railing leads to evil surmising. Once we are bent on defaming another person, we begin to look for things whether they are there or not. As Pope said, "All looks yellow to a jaundiced eye." Men become characterized by mistrust. They imagine that there is a sinister reason behind every move of a person whom they consider their adversary. They are characterized by evil surmising.

This leads to perverse disputing. They will glare at one another or smolder within. Underneath they will boil. They are vengefully nettled, convulsively agitated, thirsting for blood. The two men rub each other the wrong way. The atmosphere is one of scurrilous abuse, stinging insult, and heated invective. There will be constant covert insinuation, malicious innuendo, and thinly-veiled disdain. What started off in envy will culminate in perverse disputing.

But be aware where all this originated. It originated in minds which are corrupt, in people who are devoid of the truth. God gave these men intellectual faculties in order that they might come to the truth, but that intellectual faculty has become so depraved, so corrupt, that now it abides in a continuing state of depravity which cannot even grasp the truth. It is a mind which is completely and permanently separated from the truth of God. Hence their whole bent, rather than being one of godliness, is one of ungodliness. Error is not only unhealthy; it is ungodly.

Error Is Unprofitable (v. 5b)

The Bible teaches that godliness with contentment is great gain, but these men suppose that gain is godliness. They are so completely occupied with themselves and their own interests there is no time for God and His revealed truth. What has assumed the place of deity in

The Errors of False Teaching   113

the lives of these men is money. For the sake of becoming rich, they teach in the realm of theology.

It is very important to notice that these men are not merely deriving their livelihood from theology, or lack thereof, but they are striving to become rich through this means. They charge exorbitant fees for their instruction which they impart. They use their religious profession as a cloak for material advancement. They imagine that religion is a paying concern. But as we will see later in the chapter, true godliness is never to be commercialized, and true godliness is a matter of the heart and not the pocket.

Therefore, as verse 7 will reveal, godliness by itself is enough for the true man of God. His goal is not one of financial enhancement, but one of spiritual advancement. Therefore, to have godliness is to be rich. But to be rich, and rich alone, is to be bankrupt.

Men must understand that this kind of behavior does not in the final analysis pay; it costs. To prove to these men that it does cost, we must withdraw ourselves from them. Certainly people who treat matters of theology like this must understand that if it costs them nothing else, it costs them the fellowship of those of us who authentically redeemed. Error must be seen to be unprofitable.

CHAPTER FIFTEEN

Money Matters, Or Does It?

I Timothy 6:6-10

Paul has finished showing us that money is of primary concern to false teachers. That being the case, true Christians need to be alert lest they adopt similar attitudes. So what Paul does in this section is warn us of some of the dangers of materialism and lay down some principles about money which should help us in our everyday affairs.

The Christian life is a life of self-control (v. 6)

The truly Godly person is not interested in becoming rich. He is interested in becoming godlier. Jesus told of a farmer who made his chief goal in life the accumulation of material possessions (Luke 12:16-21). As Jesus put it, this man was laying up treasure for himself, but he was not rich toward God. Jesus said concerning this man that he was a fool. When we are concerned with accumulating gold, rather than godliness, we are foolish.

The Bible says that godliness is primarily what we need, and if we have godliness, we should be content with that. The word translated "content" is the Greek word *autarkeia*, and it is a very interesting word. It comes from two Greek words. The first is *arkeo* which was used of having sufficient strength, of being strong enough for a particular task. The second word, *autos*, means "self." So, the word literally means "to have enough strength

115

within oneself." We ought to have enough strength within ourselves to say no to the alluring things of this world. We ought to have enough strength within ourselves to be satisfied with a godly life.

This is no easy task. Contentment is not something that comes naturally to individuals. No one is born naturally content. Contentment is something which needs to be learned (cf. Philippians 4:11), something which needs to be developed in the life of the individual. The only way that contentment can be learned is for a person to be filled with the Holy Spirit. Self-control, temperance, the ability to say no to certain things is a fruit of the Spirit (Galatians 5:22-23).

It is only by placing our lives under the control of the Holy Spirit that we will be able to see that if we have godliness, we have enough. The Christian life is comprised of denying self. It is a life of understanding that if we have Jesus we have enough. Life is a constant battle of learning the secret that the Lord is our Shepherd, and that being true, we shall not want. Godliness is really all we need. To practice that, you have to be self-controlled and to be self-controlled, you have to be filled with the Spirit. There are many Christians today who are financially in a mess because they were not satisfied with spiritual things. They had to be satisfied with material things. Paul says, "Godliness with contentment is great gain." The Christian life is a life of self-control.

Financial consumption is an exercise of futility (v. 7)

The thought that is contained here is a thought that is expressed several times in Scripture. Job was one of the most righteous men in the entire Bible. The Bible says that Job was perfect and upright, a man that feared God and eschewed evil. Part of the reason that Job was able to maintain this level of righteousness even when all his material possessions were taken away was because Job had learned this principle (Job 1:21). He brought nothing into this world, and he will take nothing of this world with him when he goes. In other words, though Job owned possessions, those possessions never owned him.

Now if Job was a man who was content with whatever he had, Solomon was a man who had a very difficult time learning contentment. Solomon not only owned possessions; those possessions owned him. But notice what Solomon said at the end of his life (Ecclesiastes 5:15-16). He said, "When I leave this world, I am not going to be able to carry one single thing in my hand. I am going to leave this world the same way I came in—naked. So what did it profit me to accumulate all these possessions? They will amount to nothing when I stand at the judgment bar of God. My lifelong pursuit of material possessions was an exercise in futility; it is to be compared to chasing the wind."

Oh that we would learn this! A child is never born holding the keys to a Mercedes Benz and I have never seen a hearse pull a U-haul. You will stand before God stripped of all your material possessions. The only thing that will matter in that day is the spiritual state of your soul. Material possessions are irrelevant when you enter this world, and they are irrelevant when you exit it. There are many people who have amassed this world's goods. But in the eyes of God these people are poor and naked (cf. Revelation 3:17). They are destitute spiritually. Remember what God told the rich farmer? "This night thy soul shall be required of thee; then whose shall those things be which thou hast provided?" That night when your soul is required of you, the night of your death, material possessions will amount to nothing. That lifelong accumulation of this world's goods will be nothing more than a futile exercise.

Money is merely a means to an end (v. 8)

The word here translated "raiment" in verse 7 is the Greek word which means "covering." It refers both to covering the body with clothes and to covering the body with shelter. In other words, Paul says that as long as we have the necessities of life (food, clothing, and shelter), we should be content.

Money is necessary for these things. You need money to buy food; God doesn't want you to starve. You need money to buy clothing; you can't run around naked. You need money to buy shelter; you can't live on the street. God is not opposed to you working to buy the necessities of life. But the necessities of life (food, clothing, and shelter) are only a means to an end. Je-

Money Matters, Or Does It?

sus taught that the world for which we live is the world to come (Matthew 5:19-21). This is where our heart should be; this is where our treasure should be. The world to come should be our focus of attention. We cannot be divided in loyalty between this world and the kingdom of God. We can't serve two masters. Therefore, our primary concern should not be what we are going to eat or what we are going to wear. Our primary concern should be the kingdom of God. The food that we eat is to strengthen our body for the work of God's kingdom, and the clothes that we wear should be appropriate to advance God's kingdom. The home where we rest is necessary so the next day we can advance God's kingdom. But the focus is always the kingdom.

God gave me a car, not as a status symbol, but to be used in the work of the kingdom. God gave me a house, not to be used as a status symbol, but to be used in the work of the kingdom. Therefore, I am not to be concerned with living a life of extravagance so that people will be impressed with me. I am to be content with whatever necessities I have in order that the kingdom of God might be advanced. We are strange people. We buy things that we don't need with money that we don't have to impress people that we don't like. God says that all we need are the necessities which enable us to carry on the work of God. If I am not content with such things as I have, I reveal that my primary concern is not the advancement of God's kingdom; it is the advancement of my own kingdom. Money is not an end in and of itself. I do not work merely to gain money; I work to gain money in order that I might do the work of God. Every Christian, really, ought to be like the Apostle Paul and view his profession, whether it is tent-making or whatever, as a means of making money so that the cause of God might be advanced without charging the church. Money is merely a means to that end.

When money becomes the goal of life, we have set ourselves up for danger (vv. 9-10)

In these verses, Paul condemns materialism with the strongest words imaginable. When we are controlled by the passion to increase material possessions, we are condemned by the Word of God. It is important to note that Paul is not condemning material possessions; he is condemning the passion to increase material possessions. He is not condemning being rich; he is condemning the desire to be rich, a desire felt by both rich and poor people. If the desire of your heart is ever to grasp for more, these verses are talking about you.

When you want to obtain more, and your life has that as its goal, you will fall into a trap. It is interesting that this word *snare* is used two other times in the Pastoral Epistles, and both times the snare is described as the devil's snare. I believe this is the inference here because of the word's close association with the word *temptation*. The devil wants to trap people through the desire to accumulate worldly goods.

The temptation to be rich grabs hold of a person and imprisons him just like an animal. That desire wraps its

Money Matters, Or Does It?

tentacles around you, and it is not a grip from which you can easily free yourself.

Notice the progression. First, there is the temptation which baits the trap. Satan will dangle certain things in front of us just like a lure. It might be a new car, a new home, and nicer clothes, whatever, but we become convinced that our life will not be complete until we acquire that particular object. This is the temptation which baits the trap.

That temptation leads to lust. Lust is desire or craving. And notice carefully that once we succumb to this attitude, it is not isolated. We fall into many lusts. Once selfishness takes hold of us, it begins to manifest itself in all kinds of avenues. We think, "Well, if I get this, I will be satisfied", but we get it, and it doesn't satisfy us. So we think, "Well, I need one more thing to be satisfied." So, we get one more thing, but it doesn't satisfy us. One more thing leads to one more thing which leads to one more thing. Lust is never committed as lust (singular); it is always committed as lusts (plural). Selfishness is an attitude which covers life across the board. The lure always leads to many lusts.

But never forget that these lusts are foolish and hurtful. There is only one desire that results in our benefit, and that is the desire for godliness. Any other desire which may consume us is foolish. In the final analysis, it will not help us; it will not benefit us. It was a futile desire; hence, it was a foolish desire. This is why God told the rich young farmer, "Thou fool, this night thy soul shall be required of thee; and whose shall those things be which thou hast provided?" The accumulation of wealth as a chief pursuit is really a trivial pursuit. It is foolish.

But more importantly, it is hurtful. The temptation leads to lusts, and lusts lead to ruin. Lust when it hath conceived bringeth forth sin, and sin when it is finished bringeth forth death. So this pursuit is not only a foolish pursuit; it is a hurtful pursuit. It is a pursuit which will drown you.

How many people today are literally overwhelmed with debt? Materialism is a monster which plunges people into a sea of irretrievable loss. People have lost their possessions. They have lost their good name. They have lost their credit rating. Literally, their lives have been destroyed, and they are perishing all because they could not get a handle on their cravings.

The fact of the matter is that the love of money is the root of all kinds of evil. All kinds of calamitous things come upon houses, and families, and individuals because they love money too much. Think of all the damage and evil that comes about in this world because of the love that we have for money.

But even more than the damage that is done to individual men, think about the damage that is done to the cause of Christ because of this matter. Because of the desire for money, many have turned away from the faith. Instead of seeking the kingdom of God, they are seeking all these things. People have time to go shopping, but they don't have time to go to church. People have time to go shopping, but they don't have time to go on visitation. I am here to tell you that no truer statement was made than

Money Matters, Or Does It?

when Paul said, "Some have coveted after money to such a degree that they have erred from the way."

Though they have been lead away from spiritual matters like mindless dupes, they have no one to blame but themselves. They have pierced themselves through with many sorrows. The sorrow that they are experiencing is self-inflicted pain. Not only do they experience the danger of over-expenditure (v. 9), but they also experience the danger of non-spirituality (v. 10). Things have taken the place of God.

Things can't love you like God can love you. Things can't guide you like God can guide you. Things can't answer your prayers like God can answer your prayers. I am here to tell you that when the day of trouble comes, no material possession can do for you like God can. So you had better not let those things take the place of God. When you make money the goal of your life, you set yourself up for a peck of danger.

CHAPTER SIXTEEN

The Man of God

I Timothy 6:11-14

The descriptive phrase "man of God" is very important in the Bible. In Deuteronomy 33:1, Moses is called "the man of God." In II Chronicles 8:14, David is called "the man of God." In II Kings 1:9, Elijah is called a "man of God." When a person was endowed with the Holy Spirit and occupied a special place, he was called the man of God. Well, in the New Testament economy, every believer is a man of God (cf. II Timothy 3:17). Obviously, in this context, the phrase "man of God" is not being used of clergymen; it is being used of all believers. Believers are to be men of God.

Now if it is true that all believers are to be men of God, how much more is it true of those who have a position of great responsibility? Timothy was to be in every sense of the word "a man of God." Paul has just finished talking about men who were characterized by financial pursuits. But Timothy was not to be characterized by a desire for gold. Timothy was to be characterized by a desire for godliness. He was to be in every sense of the word "a man of God."

Now let's ask ourselves two questions. Number one, what is a man of God? And number two, why be a man of God? What is a man of God, and why be a man of God? Let's talk about that.

125

What Is a Man of God? (vv. 11-12)

I would describe a man of God as a man who is able to do certain things. At least four things are delineated in this text.

A man of God flees certain things (v. 11a)

As we have been going through the book of I Timothy, Paul has mentioned certain things that are to be avoided. And now he tells Timothy that if you want to be the man of God, flee these things. What things?

Well, in 4:7, Paul says, "Refuse profane and old wives fables." In other words, doctrinal error is to be avoided. The pastor if he wants to be a man of God must maintain time in the Bible and make sure that his teaching is not erroneous. He must flee false teaching.

And then in 4:11, Paul tells Timothy to be an example, and to let no man despise his youth. Timothy must flee not only false teaching; he must flee a filthy testimony. His testimony should be aboveboard. His testimony should be exemplary. He should not be characterized by a life which is open for accusation. He must flee the very thought of a filthy testimony.

Then all through chapter 5 Paul talks to Timothy about how to deal with people. There is a way that the pastor is to treat old men, and old women, and young women, and young men, and widows, and preacher boys, and business men, and working men. All these various groups have various needs, and it is the job of the pastor to pull all these people together in the work

The Man of God   127

of the Lord. Therefore, the pastor cannot be characterized by fragmentary thoughts. He cannot deal with one
pocket of the congregation to the exclusion of the other.
That is to be avoided.

Then finally, Paul talked in chapter 6 about false
teachers and their desire for financial compensation,
and Paul admonishes Timothy to avoid that financial
temptation, to avoid money as the prime motivator
of ministry. So Timothy, if you want to be the man of
God, avoid false teaching, and a filthy testimony, and
fragmentary thoughts about your people, and financial temptations. Timothy, if you want to be the man of
God, flee certain things. Run from them.

A man of God follows certain things (v. 11b)

If certain things are to be avoided, then certain
things are to be pursued. We are not merely to be separate from some things. We are to be separate unto some
things. There are some things that the man of God ought
to follow.

He ought to follow righteousness. His life ought to
conform to that which is right. His decisions should not
be made based on what is pragmatic or what he thinks
will work or what will cause the smallest skirmish, but
rather on what is right. Every day that stretches before
him, in every action that is performed, in every attitude
that is adopted, the pastor ought to ask himself this
question, "Is what I am doing right?" He ought to follow righteousness.

Second, he ought to follow godliness. His life ought

to be characterized by a general sense of piety. His thoughts, his affections, his motivations, his actions, all ought to be done with God in mind. He does what he does for God. He loves God with all his heart, soul, mind, and strength. He follows the pursuit of godliness.

Third, he follows faith. In other words, he believes the right things. This includes his doctrine. His belief system is based on the faith once-for-all delivered to the saints. Doctrine also refers to his basic decisions of life. He believes in God. He trusts God. He depends upon God. He is a man whose life is governed by the faith, and thus he remains in the faith, and is characterized as possessing faithfulness.

Fourth, he follows love. He loves God with all of his heart, and he loves his neighbor as himself. In this day when people love things and use people, how refreshing it is to find a man who uses things and loves people. Nothing more undeniably brands us as God's people more than love. Do you love people? The man of God does.

Fifth, the man of God follows patience. Being a man of God requires a lot of long-suffering. When you vow that you are going to love people, you make yourself vulnerable. People will take advantage of you. Thus, the man of God requires much patience. Charity suffereth long. How long-suffering are you?

Then finally, the man of God follows meekness. Meekness refers to submission. Submission to the Word of God, submission to the needs of others. The willingness to subordinate oneself to the level of service. The greatest people in the kingdom of God are those who know how to serve. Our churches today are characterized by all kinds of chiefs and no indians. Jesus came not to be ministered unto, but to minister. The man of God follows meekness.

The man of God fights certain things (v. 12a)

The word translated "fight" was used both of athletic competition and of military conflict. The idea is one of disciplined struggle, and the tense of the verb here shows that we are already in this struggle, and it is our moral obligation to maintain it. The Christian life is a life of battle. When God saved you, He put you in the army. You have been drafted.

The question is not therefore if God wants me to fight. The question is whether I am going to maintain the fight that I am already in. The Christian life is battle. It is an all-out war against the world, an all-out war against the devil, an all-out war against the flesh. The man of God takes to himself the whole armour of God, and with sword in hand goes forth to fight. The man of God fights certain things. The life of faith is battle. Therefore, make sure you fight valiantly. Fight the good fight of faith.

The man of God holds certain things (v. 12b)

The man of God must do more than simply caress and loosely hold eternal life. He must lay hold of it. And when the Bible speaks about eternal life, it is not merely talking about a quantity of life. It is talking about a quality of life, about that abundant living that was made possible through Jesus Christ.

When you became saved and received that eternal life, you made a public profession about it. You stood in the baptismal waters, and in the sight of many witnesses you professed a good profession. You said that God had taken your old life and had killed it. You said that the old you was permanently put away. You said that God created a new creature to take the place of the old one. You said that when Jesus died, your old man died, and when Jesus was buried, your old man was put away; that when Jesus walked out of that tomb, you were raised to walk in newness of life. That is what you professed, your faith in Jesus, your allegiance to Christ.

It was a good profession. You understood that God had called you to live life on a different plane. God called you to live differently than the way you previously had. God called you to live a quality of life that you had never experienced before. Well, if it is true that God called you to live out eternal life, then do it. Lay hold of that kind of living. Don't let people guess as to your allegiance. Lay hold of eternal life and make that quality of life your hallmark. In so doing, you will be a man of God.

Why Be a Man of God? (v. 13-14)

Now the question might arise, why be a man of God? Why must I flee certain things, and follow certain things, and fight certain things, and hold certain things? Paul gives us several reasons for doing so.

The Man of God   131

Because that's the kind of life the Father gives (v. 13a)

When Christ saved you, He had no desire to keep you the same. If He wanted you to stay the way you were, there was no reason to save you. God came not only to save you from the penalty of sin, but from the power of sin. God wants your life to be different from what it was. So Paul charges Timothy to live this kind of life and he charges him with a reference to God who quickens all things.

You were dead in trespasses and sins, and God made you alive. God gave you spiritual life. Why did God give you spiritual life? So that you would live spiritually. God wants you to live on this higher plane. That's the whole reason He gave you spiritual life. Therefore, to live spiritually is to live within the desires of God the Father. God the Father wants us to live that kind of life.

Because it's the kind of life that the Son lived (v. 13b)

If there ever was a man of God, it was our Lord Jesus Christ. There was no deterring Him from doing the will of God. Even when Jesus looked death in the face as He stood before Pontius Pilate, Jesus would not flinch from doing what God called Him to do. Peter and others in those moments of confrontation might deny God, but Jesus continued to profess the good profession. Jesus lived the Christian life perfectly, and Jesus is our example. If that is the kind of life that Jesus lived, then it is the kind of life that you and I ought to live.

Because it's the kind of life which keeps us unashamed (v. 14a)

When you take God's command seriously of living the Christian life, when you determine by God's grace to be a man of God, when you keep this commandment, you are now in a position to live life in such a way that your record will be clean. Your life will be without spot when it is lived as a man of God. No one will be able to rebuke you. There will be no defect in your life that people will be able to seize upon and shame you with. The way to have an unassailable character is to be a man of God.

Because it's the kind of life I want to be found doing when Jesus comes again (v. 14b)

Do you realize that Jesus is coming again? One day Jesus will appear on the horizon, and in that day, what kind of life do I want to be found doing? What kind of activity do I want to be engaged in? I don't want to be ashamed when Jesus comes, and I won't be if I continue being a man of God.

> Oh can we say we are ready, brother,
> Ready for the soul's bright home?
> Say will he find you and me still watching,
> Waiting, waiting when the Lord shall come?

CHAPTER SEVENTEEN

The Great God

I Timothy 6:15-21

You just can't be a Christian and not be impressed with the greatness of God. Paul certainly was impressed with the greatness of God.

> My God's a great God
> And worthy to be praised;
> My God's a great God,
> Oh praise His holy name!
>
> He made the world so great.
> He keeps me by His grace,
> And soon I'll see His face.
> My God's so great!

Now if you are impressed with the greatness of God, it will do certain things for you.

It will force an ascription of praise (vv. 15-16)

The greatest event of all the universe is the second advent of Jesus Christ. When Jesus Christ comes in power and great glory, it is going to be awesome. Earlier in this book, when Paul thought about the first advent, it caused him to break forth with a doxology (I Timothy 1:17). If thinking about the first advent causes one to break forth with praise, what is thinking about the Second Advent going to do? It is going to cause you to break forth with even more praise, for there is nothing which demonstrates the greatness of God more than that.

The Second Advent reveals that God is in control of history. When Jesus Christ reveals Himself at the appointed time, God will be seen for who He is—the great God of the universe, a God worthy of praise.

Praise Him as the Sovereign over Lords (v. 15)

The word *potentate* means "prince" or "chieftan." Frequently, in Greek the word was used of one who had delegated authority, but when you are talking about God, there is no delegated authority, for in reference to God there is no other authority from which He may derive power. He is the only potentate. His dignity, His blessedness, is an intrinsic personal quality. Hence, God has a right to do as He pleases in a way that no other person does.

Whatever titles others may bear, God alone is the real King. God alone is the real Lord. Literally, the Greek reads, "the King of those kinging and the Lord of those lording." Whatever authority man may have in this world, there is still an authority higher. In the final analysis, there is only one Potentate, and God should be praised for that sovereignty that He has over other lords.

Praise Him as the Source of Life (v. 16a)

God alone possesses immortality as an intrinsic

The Great God   135

characteristic. You and I may be privileged to receive immortality from Him, but He alone possesses it as an inherent right. God Himself is the source of all life. This immortality is the opposite of death. As a matter of fact, the word translated "immortality" is *athanasia*, deathlessness. We are talking here about a fullness of life. The only way that you and I can have eternal life is to become a partaker of this divine nature. But even then, we have merely received eternal life as one drinking from a fountain. God alone has eternal life. It belongs to His very being. He alone is the source of life. We should praise Him for that.

Praise Him as the Secret of Light (v. 16b)

The idea of life naturally leads to the idea of light. Life and light are inseparable. In Him was life, and the life was the light of men (John 1:4). Now the light of God is like the light of the sun. We need it to see by, yet we cannot directly look into it. It is intensely too brilliant. As the hymnwriter said, God lives in "light inaccessible hid from our eyes." It is a brilliance which no man can approach unto.

The point is that God is hidden to a certain decree. There is no way that you and I can evaluate God perfectly. God is beyond our human comprehension (cf. Isaiah 45:15). There is a sense in which God is hidden from human beings. No man hath seen, and no man can see God in all His magnificent brilliance. The sight would be too overwhelming. And this is as it should be. Praise God as the secret of light.

Yes, my friend, God is worthy of honor. He deserves our reverence, our esteem, our adoration. We ought to long to see God manifest Himself in power so that His will might be done, so that His enemies might be discomfited, so that His people might be saved. God is a great God. That fact alone ought to force an ascription of praise.

It will force an adjustment of priorities (vv. 17-19)

Earlier in this chapter, Paul talked about people who were aspiring to be rich. Here, however, he talks about people who are already rich. There is no denunciation here about being rich. The denunciation is about wrong priorities. If I really understand God to be a great God, it will do something about my priorities. My priority will be God, not gold.

There are two dangers that rich men must guard against. First, they must guard against being high-minded. Sometimes when people come into money they become high and mighty. Such will not be the case of the man who recognizes the greatness of God. He will understand that there is only one potentate, and it is not the human being with money. It is the God who gave him that money so that he could richly enjoy it. The golden rule is not "he who has the gold rules."

The second warning to rich men is that they not trust in uncertain riches. God alone is the source of life. God alone is the source of light. God is the source of

The Great God

eternality. Riches are certainly not that stable. Markets rise and markets fall. The dollar inflates, and the dollar deflates, but God stays always the same. Therefore, you and I should trust in the certainty of God rather than in the uncertainty of riches.

Now when I understand that money is not a god, but rather a gift from God, then I will use it wisely. When I understand that gold is not great in and of itself, but rather the God who gave me the gold is great, then I will use that money for divine purposes. My priorities will be adjusted.

I will use my money to do good things. I will be more concerned with being rich in good works than rich at the neighborhood bank. I will always be ready to distribute rather than hoard. I will always be willing to communicate rather than to ostracize. I will use my money to reach out rather than to pull in.

In so doing, I will make a deposit at the most important bank in all the universe, the bank of heaven. This is the ultimate in saving for a rainy day. We all want a good nest egg for the future, something built up on which we can fall back. Well then we had better be concerned with having something built up for that future day when we stand before God.

When we live life this way, we live life as God intended for it to be lived. This is life which is life indeed, and life will be lived that way every day when it is lived with the greatness of God in mind. The greatness of God forces us to adjust our priorities.

It will force an accuracy in preaching (vv. 20-21)

Paul here continues the metaphor of banking by telling Timothy to keep that which has been committed to his trust. Timothy is to guard the truth of God as if it were a fixed deposit. The truth of God is something that is to be preciously protected. It is like treasure placed in a bank for safekeeping, and the pastor must encourage people to come and make a withdrawal from the Gospel, but this withdrawal will only be meaningful if the pastor has protected the Gospel's purity.

If we are going to protect the purity of the Gospel, then we must turn down counterfeits. We have got to avoid profane and vain babblings. The jargon of false teachers is nothing more than futility. It is profane. It is vain. It is mere babbling. Therefore, avoid it.

It is something which only purports to be the truth, but in reality it is not truth at all. It calls itself science, but in reality it is not science. Such a tag is a misnomer. It is a false label. It is not the truth; it stands in opposition to the truth.

When people profess it, they err from the real faith, the faith which is through grace. Now all of this has wide ramifications for the pastor, and indeed for all believers. If God is indeed great, then we must see God's salvation as infinitely pre-eminent over the religions developed by men. We must zealously guard the right Gospel, and zealously oppose the false gospel. In a word, the greatness of God will make our preaching accurate.

Of course, this requires the grace of God. It requires dependency upon God lest we deviate into doctrinal er-

The Great God 139

ror. This is the grace that Paul desired for Timothy and his friends, and may that same desire be fulfilled in us. Grace be with you. Amen.

CHAPTER EIGHTEEN

The Value of Proclamation

II Timothy 1:1-2

The first thing that Paul tells us about himself in this passage is the fact that he is an apostle. The Greek word *apostellos* is actually a compound word. It comes from the word *apo* meaning "from" and the word *stello* meaning "sent." Thus, the word *apostle* literally means "one sent from." In secular Greek, the word was used of an ambassador who was sent to represent another. Thus, in the Bible, the word *apostle* is used of one sent to represent God.

In that sense, Jesus Christ was an apostle. The author of the book of Hebrews refers to Christ Jesus as an apostle (Hebrews 3:1). Indeed, no one represented God any better than Jesus did. Jesus so adequately represented God that Jesus could say, "He who has seen me has seen the Father." Jesus was the full revelation of God because in Jesus dwelt all the fullness of the Godhead bodily. Jesus was God's official representative to mankind.

When Jesus left this earth, He left behind His inner core of disciples who the Bible says He had named "apostles" (Luke 6:13). To be an apostle of Jesus Christ, certain things had to be true of you. When the apostles were looking for a replacement for Judas, Peter said that an apostle had to be a witness of the entire ministry of Jesus from the time he was baptized by John in the

Jordan River, all the way up to His resurrection (Acts 1:22). Matthias was chosen to be in the circle of the twelve apostles.

The Bible also speaks of an apostle born out of time. That was the Apostle Paul (I Corinthians 15:8-9). His apostleship was on a different plane than the apostleship of the other twelve. He had not been a witness of the entire earthly ministry of Christ. But God chose Paul "out of time" in order that he might be a special apostle to the Gentiles (Romans 11:13). So, there was a special role to Gentile people that the Apostle Paul was to play. God chose him to be an apostle out of time.

Jesus is said to be an apostle. The twelve are said to be apostles. Paul in a unique role was an apostle, but there is a wider sense in which we can say all Christians are apostles (Acts 14:4). There is a sense in which the term *apostle* can be used as a synonym for any Christian. There is a sense in which all of us have been sent to represent God. Certainly we don't come exactly as Christ came, or as the twelve came, or as the Apostle Paul came. We don't come exactly in that capacity, but there is a sense in which all Christians officially represent Jesus Christ.

If we are saved, we are official representatives of Jesus Christ. We are sent ones. God has sent us to a lost world. God has commissioned us to tell them about Himself. He has commissioned us to preach the Gospel to every creature. Why is this task is so important? Let's think about the value of proclamation.

The Value of Proclamation

Evangelism is the will of God (v. 1a)

When Paul says that he is an apostle of Jesus Christ, he means that he was commissioned by Jesus Christ. He means that Jesus Christ sent him (cf. Acts 9:6-7). Paul, on the road to Damascus, had a face-to-face encounter with Jesus. Being brought face to face with Jesus, Paul asked a very important question. "Lord, what wilt thou have me to do?" Anyone who has been brought face to face with Jesus ought to be asking that question. Have you met Jesus? If so, have you asked Jesus what He would have you to do? Jesus told Paul to go into the city, and there it would be told him what to do. Part of what God was going to unfold to the Apostle Paul was that this man was to be a chosen vessel to bear Christ's name before Gentiles, kings, and the children of Israel (Acts 9:15-16).

You have been saved. You need something to do. You have been chosen to bear Christ's name. If there was anything the Apostle Paul was sure about; it was the fact that he had been sent by Christ (Galatians 1:1). There is a tremendous consequence of being sent by Christ and that consequence is found in Galatians 1:16. When God sees fit to reveal His Son in you, this is not a matter that needs human confirmation. When God tells you to preach the Gospel among the heathen, that's all you need to know. Nobody else's word matters. God commissioned it; that settles it.

Evangelism, at its core, is so vital simply because it is the will of God (Matthew 28:18-20). Jesus Christ possesses all authority in heaven and in earth. Therefore, whatever Jesus Christ says goes, and Jesus said that you and I should be going and discipling all nations. This commission was not limited to the early apostles because Jesus said that this activity should continue right up until the end of the age. Thus, all of us have been sent by Jesus Christ. All of us know that it is the will of God for us to be going. Evangelism is important simply because it is the will of God.

Evangelism is a matter of life or death (v. 1b)

As we go out, being sent, we go offering men a promise, a promise of life (cf. Ephesians 4:18). Do you realize that every lost person has been removed from life support? Every lost person is alienated from the life of God, and the glorious truth is that you and I can go to these people and offer them the gift of life. We can promise life.

We have heard promises all of our lives. Numerous politicians of varying political parties have promised us a better standard of living. Our standard of living is not to be found in Washington D.C. That is not where I look for my promise of life.

As a sixteen-year-old child, I sat in the Hospital Room of Mansfield General Hospital, and I remember that day as if it only happened a view hours ago. The doctor looked me in the eyes and told me I had a disease which all medical books painted fatalistically. I was to gradually deteriorate and die a young death. The doctor told me there was nothing he could do. I remember the hours that followed that news. I sat on the side of that hospital bed frustrated. Here was a man that had been to medical school. He had studied diseases; he was supposed to be able to cure disease and prolong life. I looked to that man for a promise of life, and he could not give it to me.

Contrast that with the glorious words of Jesus in John 11:25-26. The words which that doctor could not give, Jesus gave. Jesus said if you are looking for life, I am it. The one who believes in me will never die. Life is not to be found in the political world. Life is not to be found in the medical world. Life is to be found in the spiritual world. Jesus Christ is the true God. Jesus Christ is eternal life (I John 5:20). If you have Jesus, you have life. If you don't have Jesus, you don't have life. Therefore, when you and I go representing Christ, we go offering people a promise of life, because life is in Christ Jesus. Jesus is not merely the joy of living; He is life itself. To offer people Jesus is to offer them spiritual life.

As a young twelve-year-old boy, I was a bus captain at my home church. My route had several different drivers. On one particular Sunday, my dad was my bus driver. We turned the corner to pick up some kids at the top of this hill, and when dad went to apply the brakes, he discovered he didn't have any. That church bus began to go down that hill gaining speed as it went. My dad tried to pull the bus into a ditch but it only bounced out, clipping mailboxes as it went. At the end of that street, the road was a dead end dropping several feet into a ravine below. There have only been a few times in my life when

I thought death was really imminent; that was one of those times. Praise the Lord, God gave my dad enough discernment to bring that bus to a stop in the only place it could have stopped safely. I am sure that if I had been driving that bus, everybody on it would have died, but somehow, some way my father was able to bring that bus to safety.

Your life is on a dead-end street, racing toward destruction. Along that road of life, you have bounced from one thing to another, and nothing has helped. You know that as long as you are at the wheel, your life is headed for death. Isn't it about time you let the Father take the wheel? Only He can bring you to a place of safety. Only He can steer your life in the right direction. Only He can save your life.

Sadly, many will not come to Jesus in order that they might have life (John 5:40). Oh, how that ought to concern us! Without Christ, men are without life. Evangelism is a matter of life and death.

Evangelism is a means of establishing fellowship (v. 2a)

Have you noticed that saved people and lost people don't think the same? The fact of the matter is that righteousness does not have any fellowship with unrighteousness (cf. II Corinthians 6:14-17). A child of God cannot have close, intimate fellowship with a lost person. It just cannot happen unless you make some compromises. Here, then, is part of the reason for evange-

The Value of Proclamation   147

lism. If light has no fellowship with darkness, then our job is to take light to those who are in the dark, and if they embrace the light, then we can have fellowship (I John 1:3). We preach the Gospel for the sake of establishing fellowship.

There is no greater fellowship than the fellowship that exists in the body of Christ. When Paul described the fellowship that existed between himself and Timothy, he put it on the level of a father and a son. Timothy was dearly beloved just as if he were Paul's own child.

When our daughters came home upset, there was nobody more sensitive to that than their mother and me. When they are being praised, we are as proud as can be. When they are being ridiculed, there is no one hurt more than we are. I am saying that their pains are our pains, and their joys are our joys. Our lives are inextricably woven into theirs, that whatever happens to them happens to us at the same time. They are our children.

Paul picks up this truth to drive home the fact that there is a bond that exists in the body of Christ which no outsider can understand.

> When one has a heartache,
> We all share the tear,
> And rejoice in each victory
> In this family so dear.

When you become saved, you receive a brand new family. There is a family stronger than the family of blood; it is the family of faith (cf. Matthew 12:49-50).

Especially when you have the privilege of leading

someone to the Lord, you become interested in his or her life. If you have never brought another person into the world spiritually, how can I describe it you? It is just as difficult as describing motherhood to a woman who has never had a baby. The only way you can know the feeling is to experience it. There is no other way to know the intimate fellowship that can be established. Oh, the joy of having a dearly beloved child!

Evangelism is a means of bestowing benefit (v. 2b)

Our world is a world that is constantly talking about peace. In the sixties, we used to hold up two fingers and say, "Peace, man." We sang, "Let there be peace on earth, and let it begin with me." We have talked about ways to achieve peace. Do we build our arsenals to have peace through strength, or do we advocate nuclear disarmament? On the local level, do we ban guns? Or do we believe that if guns are outlawed, only outlaws will have guns? There is a lot of debate that wages in the public sector about ways to achieve peace.

This not only occurs with regard to external peace; it occurs with regard to internal peace. Many people are dissatisfied with their jobs, dissatisfied with their looks, dissatisfied with their spouse. We live in a world that is extremely uptight. There is much talk about the acquisition of internal peace. Psychologists and counselors have offered their various suggestions as to how mankind can become one with himself. We are searching for an elusive state of peace.

The Value of Proclamation

In addition, there have been wide-ranging discussions about the best way to be merciful. Some people would say that the best way to be merciful is to give someone a fish to eat. Another person would say, "No, if you give a person a fish you have only helped him for a day, but if you teach a person how to fish, you have helped him for life." Does welfare help people, or does welfare ultimately harm people? In what way can we best be merciful?

Paul gives us a clue in verse two when he presents a triad of benefits in a sequential order. If you and I are to know peace, we must receive mercy, which stems from grace. But we are not talking here about just any grace. We are talking about the grace of God the Father which is mediated through the person of Christ Jesus our Lord. Jesus was the Messiah. He was the anointed one of whom the Old Testament spoke. This Messiah came to be our Savior. But this Messiah not only came to be our Savior; He also came to be our Lord. When a person asks Christ to save his soul placing himself under the authority of Christ, he receives the grace of God which is able to bestow mercy and peace.

We are often perplexed about the best way to help society. Should we try to save the whales, protect the ozone, or recycle? What significant contribution can I make to the betterment of mankind? Let me suggest the ultimate way you may be a benefactor. Do the work of an evangelist. When you bring the grace of God in the person of Christ to a lost world, you are doing the most merciful act that can be done. You are making the most significant contribution to world peace that can be made. Because mercy and peace are found in the gracious act of introducing people to God the Father through the Lord Jesus Christ, what greater contribution can we make than this?

Sinful and lonely and dying,
Wand' ring far in the night,
Waiting, longing for someone
To lead them to Christ and the light.

This is the ultimate kindness,
This is love at its best;
Sharing Jesus with others;
From the north, south, the east and the west.

Share Jesus with others;
He loves and will save them too.
Share Jesus with others;
That's what a Christian should do.

CHAPTER NINETEEN

Making a Man of God

II Timothy 1:3-8

Timothy's very name means "honored of God." Out of all the friends of the Apostle Paul, none perhaps stands out as vividly as his young pastor friend, Timothy. The book of II Timothy is the last letter that Paul would write which would become a part of Scripture. This letter bears Timothy's name. Why? Because even at the end of his life, the Apostle Paul was interested in Timothy and had faith that the ministry of Timothy would flourish. Paul really believed that Timothy would amount to something.

As we approach death, we give much consideration to the past. You will notice in verse three that Paul speaks about his forefathers. In verse five, he speaks about Timothy's mother and grandmother. But people who are approaching death not only think of the past; they think of the future as well. Paul's future was invested in Timothy. Here was a man that would continue the things that the Apostle Paul had started (cf. 2:2).

It is important for an Apostle Paul to have a Timothy. It is important for the elderly to look to a few, good, younger men who are continuing the things they started. It is good for a parent to see his or her children continuing in the faith. Every mother should want a son like Timothy. How does a mother make a man of God like this?

151

A man of God is made by supplication (v. 3)

If there is one thing I know about the Apostle Paul, it is the fact that he believed in prayer. Paul without ceasing prayed for the church at Rome (Romans 1:9). Paul told the church at Colossae that he always prayed for them (Colossians 1:3). Here for the young pastor Timothy, Paul says, "Without ceasing I have remembered you in my prayers night and day." Part of what made Timothy a man that you could be thankful for was the fact that a mentor had been praying fervently. In the morning and in the evening, habitually, Timothy was prayed for.

The Apostle Paul says that God's people ought to be characterized by prayer (II Thessalonians 5:17). Pray without ceasing, he says. Certainly when we go to prayer, we should remember to pray for our children. Job, the most righteous man who ever lived apart from the Lord Jesus, prayed continually for his children (Job 1:5). Who knows what temptations our children will face today? Who knows what lurks within their depraved hearts? Is this not reason to pray for them?

> Did you think of us this morning
> As you breathed a word of prayer?
> Did you ask for strength to help us
> All our heavy burdens bear?
>
> Someone prayed, and strength was given
> For the long and weary road,
> Someone prayed and faith grew stronger
> As we bent beneath our load.

Making a Man of God 153

Someone prayed -- the way grew brighter,
And we walked all unafraid.
In our heart a song of gladness
Tell me, was it you who prayed?

Ah, mother in the day of busy activity, I know there are clothes to wash, meals to prepare, rooms to clean, and countless other things that go with mothering. But let nothing take the place of the time you must pray for your children. A man of God is made when without ceasing, night and day, we have remembered him in prayer. A man of God is made by supplication.

A man of God is made by sensation (v. 4)

Timothy was a man of God who was sensitive. Paul greatly desired to see this. Every time that he came in contact with Timothy, he was filled with joy. Why? Because Timothy was a man who knew how to cry. So often Paul had met with opposition to the things of God. Even as he wrote this letter, he was in a harsh prison cell awaiting execution. Paul, throughout his entire ministry, encountered harshness, but in Timothy there was an uncommon sensitivity. He was sensitive to sin, sensitive to the moving of the Spirit of God. That's why Paul was greatly desiring to see him. That's why Paul was filled with joy at every encounter he had with Timothy. Here was a man who was sensitive.

Sometimes, I believe, we want different things in men than God wants. We want men who can face up to winds, earthquakes, and fires. God wants men who are sensitive to that still, small voice (II Kings 19:9-13). The modern era has taught us differently.

> Don't cry out aloud; keep it inside
> Learn how to hide your feelings.
> Fly high and proud, and if you should fall,
> Remember you almost had it all.

The Bible, however, states, "Jesus wept", and here is where mom's influence is imperative. Teach that boy to be sensitive to sin. Teach that boy to be sensitive to the Holy Spirit of God.

> I want a principle within
> Of watchful, godly fear.
> A sensibility of sin,
> A pain to feel it near.
> Help me the first approach to feel
> Of pride or wrong desire;
> To catch the wandering of my will,
> And quench the kindling fire.
>
> From Thee that I no more may stray,
> No more Thy goodness grieve,
> Grant me a child-like faith, I pray,
> A tender conscience give;
> Quick as the focus of an eye,
> O God, my conscience make!
> Awake my soul when sin is nigh,
> And keep it still awake.

We are raising a generation of children that are "past feeling" (cf. Epheisans 4:19). Thus, they have giv-

Making a Man of God   155

en themselves over to sins of all sort. There are many around us who tell lies and live hypocritically because their consciences are seared (I Timothy 4:2). Their nerve endings are dead. The weeping prophet lamented the fact that no one blushed at sin (Jeremiah 6:15). So, while we are raising kids to be stoic, God is looking for men who are sensitive. A man of God is made by sensation.

A man of God is made by salvation (v. 5)

The reason that we pray fervently for a child and by discipline make him sensitive to sin is all for a single purpose. And that purpose is salvation. We want unfeigned faith, that is, unhypocritical or genuine faith in that child. Now how do we do this? First, we must make sure that this kind of faith is in us. Notice that Paul says this unfeigned faith was first in his grandmother Lois, and then in his mother Eunice, and then in Timothy also.

I don't want to be satisfied with my child simply making a profession of faith. I want to see some validity behind that profession. I don't want my child to profess Christ, but in works deny Him. I want my child's faith to be unfeigned. I don't want to be snowed with regard to my child's salvation. I don't want my child to be a hypocrite.

So, the first thing that I must do is must make sure that I am not a hypocrite. If I want unfeigned faith in my child, then let me first make sure that I have unfeigned faith in me. Particularly in the home, people learn much by way of observation (cf. I Peter 3:1-2). If you are preaching the Bible all the time, but not living it, it doesn't accomplish as much. Those within the home many times are won by watching our behavior. They must behold our chaste behavior coupled with fear. Nothing will turn a child off to Christianity any quicker than a hypocritical parent. What is the prerequisite for teaching your children? First, you have got to make sure that it is in your heart (Deuteromony 6:4-7). Only then are you adequately qualified to teach your kids. Dear parent, if you don't live holy, your kids won't see the Lord (cf. Hebrews 12:14). No person can be made into a man of God until first he becomes saved, and that salvation all begins when we as parents determine to live right.

A man of God is made by stimulation (vv. 6-7)

We have taken this child, and we have prayed for him. We have paddled him making him sensitive to sin. We have seen him pardoned through salvation. Now once we have supplication, sensation, and salvation, what comes next? Stimulation! Wherefore, that is, because he has real faith, we need to remind him to stir up the gift of God which is in him. The phrase "stir up" was a fire term. It carries with it the idea of kindling afresh by stirring up the embers.

If a child is genuinely saved, he has more than just natural abilities and talents. He actually has the supernatural operation of the Holy Spirit resident within his person. He possesses *charismata* (the gift), and that gift

Making a Man of God   157

is in him. This is not an external operation; this is an internal grace. In Timothy's case, that grace was recognized the day he was ordained to the Christian ministry, when the Apostle Paul laid hands on him. The very fact that Timothy was commissioned to preach the Gospel at his ordination meant that God had provided the wherewithal to get that commission accomplished.

So now Paul comes to Timothy and encourages him to get on with that commission. After all, God has not given us the spirit of timidity. At his ordination, Timothy was not given a spirit of cowardice. The Gospel cannot be furthered by men of craven spirit. Just the opposite is true.

God has given us the spirit of power, that is, the strength of character needed to be bold in the exercise of authority. The spirit of power within a man has led many ministers who were naturally timid to develop a boldness not their own. When I was a child, I was very timid. I ran around hiding, with my finger in my mouth, crying at the least amount of embarrassment. But from my ordination on, God has given me spirit of power. It is not my own. I take no credit for it.

Second, God gave Timothy a spirit of love. This is a characteristic indispensable to any Christian, but especially to Christian ministers. Paul understood the difference a love for people could make in the ministry. Read I Corinthians 13 if you have any doubt about that.

Then God gave Timothy the spirit of a sound mind. Ministers ought to have a level head. There is a constant Satanic assault upon the mind of a pastor. You miss budget a couple of weeks and the devil convinces you that the people are trying to starve you out. Someone misses church for a couple of services and the devil convinces you that you are the reason why. It is a constant battle to stay sound in your thinking. We are so given to irrational and illogical deductions. Especially, if you are naturally timid like Timothy, you see a demon behind every rock.

So, Paul comes to Timothy and encourages him. He stimulates him in the right direction. Don't be timid. Rather, stir up in yourself what you were ordained to do. Use the spirit of ministry. Keep on being powerful. Keep on loving the people. Keep on thinking straight. Oh what power there is at a parent's disposal to channel their kids properly by the right kind of stimulation! Constantly be there, and constantly admonish them to keep on in the things of God. It is your duty, dear parent, to be a Christian cheerleader. That's what you are there for.

If I am not there stimulating my kids to do the right things, then you had better believe that there will be someone there stimulating them to do the wrong things. Therefore, with every fiber of my being, I must remind them to stir up the gift of God. I have got to stimulate them to good works.

Men of God are made by security (v. 8)

Now let's say a child has been prayed for, and let's say that child is raised to be sensitive to sin and the Spirit. Let's say the child gets saved and let's say the child is

Making a Man of God   159

encouraged to go on with the Lord. What comes next? We must prepare that child for opposition. Whenever a child has a testimony for the Lord, there will be a price to pay. There is a bondage, an imprisonment that goes with the Gospel. Whenever you partake of the Gospel with fervency, there will be affliction.

I don't care whether your child is in the public school, or the Christian school, or in a home school fellowship, not every child that your child associates with will be spiritual. If your child takes a stand for God, he will be laughed at, he will be ridiculed, and there will be a price to pay.

Some because of the stress of peer pressure will become ashamed of the Lord. It is our job as parents to prevent that from happening. The way we prevent that from happening is by teaching that child to depend upon the power of God. For if that child is depending upon the power of God, he will be able to withstand the affliction. He will be able to take it, yea to actually partake of it, because the power of God operating within in his person is stronger than the peer pressure from without.

You cannot possibly be with your child everywhere in every place. Try as you may to shelter your child, there will come a day when that child will have to stand alone on his own two feet. Therefore, the child's ability to stand must not come predominantly from a smothering parent, but rather from an intestinal fortitude provided by nobody less than God Himself.

Isn't that the job of us as parents, anyway? Isn't it

our job to teach our kids how to stand alone on their own two feet? If I raise my children to be perpetually dependent upon me, I have failed. That child must face this ungodly world head on (cf. Philippians 2:15-16). I want them to be so secure in their faith that they are not ashamed of it, but rather are strong enough to partake of the affliction associated with the Gospel. It is my job as a parent to provide them with that security.

Oh, parents; have you stopped to think
You hold a sacred place?
That child of yours, will he thank God
You told him of God's grace?
Or will the future have to be,
Where is my child today?
Because you had no thought of God,
You lived for self your way.

You did not do things very bad,
You had no time to pray.
You do have time for worldly things
But none for God today.
You lead your child the way you go,
For self at any cost:
Then find out when it is too late
Your child and you are lost.

How comforting it is to know
You taught your child to pray,
To read the blessed Word of God
And live for God each day.
By word and life to love God's house
For worship, prayer, and praise,
Until you meet with all the saved

Making a Man of God

For everlasting days.
How wonderful to fellowship
With Christ the risen Lord,
With all the family saved by grace
Rejoicing in God's Word.
For mother sang each child to sleep
With hymns of love and grace.
With joy they wait for Christ's return
To meet Him face to face.

The man who has a Christian wife
Has found a treasure rare,
A mother for his children's good
Who nurtures them with prayer.
So mother, if you know the Lord,
Live close to Him each day.
In every problem that you face
Let Jesus lead the way.

CHAPTER TWENTY

I am Saved; Now What?

II Timothy 1:9-18

I like the first four words of verse nine. The "who" refers to God. (v. 8) God hath saved us. There are many terms used to describe what happened to us when we became Christians. We became justified, regenerated, sanctified, adopted, redeemed, but perhaps no word better encompasses all other terms than the word *salvation*. Have you ever been saved? Have you ever let God save you from your sins, from yourself, from hell? Do you know what it means to be saved? I trust that you do. But once a person becomes saved, what then? I am saved; now what?

The Consequences of Salvation (vv. 9-10)

Death has been abolished (v. 10b)

Many times when Paul speaks of death, he speaks of it having been abolished (cf. I Corinthians 15:26). Do you know that death is an enemy? Death separates loved ones from each other. Death leaves people lonely. Death is feared by many people. Death is an enemy, but Paul says in I Corinthians that death will be destroyed. The word translated "destroyed" is the same word translated "abolished" in II Timothy 1:10. In I Corinthians 15:26, Paul says death will be abolished, but in II Timothy 1:10, he uses an aorist tense and says that death already

163

has been abolished. There is no contradiction. Death has been abolished through the death of Jesus Christ. Jesus Christ died so that death may die. In I Corinthians, Paul is speaking about the consummation of that which has already been accomplished through Christ's atoning work. So, though we wait for the consummation of death's destruction, we can say just as forcefully as Paul did in II Timothy that death already has been abolished for the Christian.

So, if Jesus Christ has abolished death, then you and I have nothing to fear (Hebrews 2:14-15). Previous to conversion, death was a fearful thing. It was something to be dreaded, but not anymore. Death has no more sting (I Corinthians 15:55). The grave has no more victory. For the person who is saved, death has been abolished.

Life and immortality are illuminated (v. 10c)

Frequently, God uses terms like *darkness* and *blindness* to describe those who are without Christ. The fact of the matter is that men love darkness rather than light because their deeds are evil. But those of us who are saved are described by the Bible as being children of the light. We are illuminated individuals, and if there is anything concerning which we have been illuminated, it is this whole matter of living.

The sad thing is most people on the street have absolutely no concept of what it means to really live, and when they talk about really living, or living life to the full, or living it up, they are usually referring to some

I am Saved; Now What? 165

type of sinful activity. They usually use these terms to describe an event or an act that brings decay, disease, and dissatisfaction. Thus, to many people, living is nothing more than giving to oneself lung cancer, liver disease, or aids. Obviously, such people know nothing about living; they are still in the dark.

When God saved us through the Gospel message, this whole matter of how to live was brought to light. Living is not comprised of self-injury. Living rather, if it is done in accordance with God's Word, is a life that is characterized by immortality. Thus, whenever the Bible speaks of life, or everlasting life, or eternal life, it is doing much more than speaking of a duration of life. After all, everybody is going to live forever some place. Rather, the Bible is speaking about a quality of life, a life void of destruction, void of dissatisfaction, a life of immortality. Saved people are people who have been illuminated concerning life.

Holiness is called for (vv. 9-10a)

Now as Christians, we have the opportunity to live a life not characterized by death but rather characterized by life and immortality. But this is not only our opportunity; this is our obligation. At the very moment God saved us, He also called us. So, in the Bible, there is always a close connection between salvation and vocation. Christians are not only saved from a life of sin, but they are called to a life of holiness. God has called us with a holy calling. In other words, God wants to produce His holiness in our lives once we are saved, and that is precisely what He has called us to do.

When we set out on this course of holiness, we must recognize that we will never be able to produce holiness through our efforts and ingenuity. Just as no one is able to save himself, so no one is able to sanctify himself. Sanctification is not according to our own human works. If we are going to be sanctified, it must be done according to the purpose of God through the grace of God. In other words, if we are going to be sanctified, we need God's help and the help of God is to be found in the person of the Lord Jesus Christ. God has called us to be holy. That is His purpose for us, but if we are to fulfill that purpose, we must utilize His grace which is found in the person of Jesus.

Before the world even began, God knew that man would fall and that man would never be able to make himself holy. Therefore, even before the world began, God made provision for our holiness. The provision for our holiness is found in the Lord Jesus Christ. This is one of the premier reasons Jesus appeared on planet earth. The God-man appeared as our Savior in order that holiness might be manifested in you and me. Now as Christians, God calls us to utilize that holiness found in the person of Jesus.

The Charge to the Saved (vv. 11-14)

A Practical Charge (v. 11)

If you and I really believe that God does abolish the sentence of death that hangs over people's heads, and

I am Saved; Now What?   167

if we really do believe that God brings to light a non-corrupted way of living, and if we really do believe that God is calling for holiness in our lives, then we had better do something about it. God has already done something about it. Before the foundation of the world, God determined that Jesus would come to be the source of holiness.

Now God comes to you and me, as Christians, and He says, "I need you to proclaim this message for me." God says, "I have appointed you a preacher. You are My sent one. You are one that I have appointed to teach the heathen." Thus, the first step of the calling toward holiness is a call to take the message of the Gospel to a lost world. They are in death. They don't know how to live. They have no concept of God's holiness. Thus, God has appointed you and me to preach and teach it. It is a very practical charge.

I know that Paul here is talking about his technical, vocational calling as a preacher, apostle, and teacher. But let us not think that the average laymen has not been called, is not to preach, is not to go, is not to teach the unregenerate. The charge is very practical. They have never heard of Jesus. You and I must let them know.

A Personal Charge (v. 12)

When you start to fulfill your calling and take the Gospel to the heathen, many times you will not be readily received. There is much to suffer for the cause of Christ. The one who takes the Gospel must expect a hostile reaction from many. Look at what they did with Jesus Himself. Do we delude ourselves into thinking that the message concerning Christ will be treated any differently than Christ Himself was treated? For the cause of evangelism, we will suffer some things.

But let us not be ashamed of that suffering. After all, though they may treat us roughly because of our affiliation with Him, we know whom we have believed. I like the fact that Paul does not say, "I know what I have believed." Rather, he says, "I know whom I have believed." Paul's faith was more than belief in a rote creed. He had trusted the ever-living One. That day when Paul was saved, when he committed his life to God, Paul did more than believe some facts about the Gospel. Paul went further than that. He committed his soul to God Himself.

Whatever you commit to God, God is able to keep. He is able to keep it right up unto the day we meet Him face to face. Be persuaded of that fact. The point then is that God is never going to give up on you. He is going to safe guard your soul that has been committed to His care. If God then is never ashamed of you, but rather keeps you with diligent care, why should you ever be ashamed of Him? So the charge goes way beyond the practicality of doing the job; it extends to you personally as to motive. Are you ashamed of Jesus or are you proud of Him? He is keeping on with you, why don't you keep on with Him?

A Propositional Charge (vv. 13-14)

Now when we were saved, we committed our souls

I am Saved; Now What?

to God, but at the same time, God committed something to us. God committed to us a propositional body of truth. And these sound words which God gave us must be rigorously held to. Paul here provided an example for Timothy to follow. The way Paul preached was a form or an example for Timothy to trace. Every preacher is to be a doctrinal preacher.

I remember once back home our church wanted to start a nursing home ministry at a particular facility. And the activities director of that nursing home asked my preacher, "You are not going to preach doctrine, are you?" If you are not preaching doctrine, you have nothing to preach. What Timothy heard from the lips of Paul was sound words, and that form was to be copied.

Now as we hold to an orthodox position, there is an attitude that is to accompany our orthodoxy. Orthodoxy has an orthopraxy. First, doctrine is to be held with faith. In other words, we are commanded to really believe what the Bible says. We are not to apologize on behalf of God or on behalf of ourselves for believing what God says. Hold an orthodox position in faith. But at the same time, hold an orthodox position in love. In other words, speak the truth in love. Don't love so much you fail to speak the truth, and don't speak the truth so much you fail to love. Speak the truth in love. Hold sound words in faith and in love. That balance is necessary, and it is possible.

Jesus had it. Jesus was full of grace and truth. And since this same Jesus lives in us, and we are in Him, we can have the same balance. As Paul says in verse fourteen, the Holy Ghost dwells in us, enabling us to keep the right position in the right way. And therefore, we can keep sound words because the power to do so lives inside of us.

The Contention against the Saved (vv. 15-18)

Whenever you hold the truth, even if you hold the truth in love, you can expect people to turn away from you. And sometimes this turning away reaches epidemic proportions. Paul said, "All Asia turned away from me." Now of course, this was hyperbole, but it does seem sometimes that the entire world will have nothing to do with us.

And of this mass that turned away from Paul, two particular fellows really hurt. They were Phygellus and Hermogenes. Probably, these two fellows were the main cause of the trouble. As one looks back on pastoral ministry, most of it has been good, but there are always those two or three that have given some trouble. Sometimes, these two or three can be so demonstrative they make you think the whole world is after you. Just two or three can be responsible for a sweeping all-encompassing depression.

Because there will always be contention against those who have the courage to hold the truth, the Christian church is in desperate need of people like Onesiphorus. Onesiphorus was the type of man who did not doubt Paul. He did not say, "I wonder what Paul did to have people treat him so rough." Onesiphorus was not ashamed of Paul's chain. He made a point to look for hurting people

I am Saved; Now What?   171

and find them. Paul says, "He oft refreshed me."

Because Paul had received so much mercy from Onesiphorus, it was Paul's prayer that the Lord would repay that mercy to his entire house. When you stand before God in that day, how do you want God to treat you? Do you want God to treat you with rote barren justice? Or do you want God to treat you with mercy? We ought to treat people the way we want God to treat us. When people look at the saints of this area, my desire is that the people of this town would know many things we have done to the hurting Christians of our town. May they know that very well.

CHAPTER TWENTY-ONE

The Value of Perseverance

II Timothy 2:1-26

Later, we will look at the value of peril. This age will be characterized by perilous times. If this age is characterized by perilous times, then obviously we can expect defections. Indeed, in 1:15, Paul said that this very thing had happened. Some of the Asians had turned away from apostolic instruction. Now in light of these defections, the Apostle Paul turns to Timothy and says, "You, my son, need to be strong. You need to keep on persevering in the work of the Lord." So now we look at the value of perseverance.

The Source of Perseverance (v. 1)

If a person is to persevere, he must persevere in the grace that is in Christ Jesus. This emphatically implies the ability to persevere is found solely in Christ. It is not to be found in human effort; rather, it is to be found in divine grace. Grace in this context refers to divine help, the unmerited gift of assistance that comes from God. The times are so perilous that if we are to be strong, we must be strong in the grace that is in Christ Jesus.

Now if this grace, this help, is found in Christ Jesus, then every single Christian possesses it and can rely upon it. If this strength to persevere is found in Christ Jesus, and I have Christ Jesus, then I have the ability to persevere. No Christian can truthfully say, "I just

173

couldn't help myself." Yes, we can, because we have the power supply, the grace resident within us in the person of Jesus Christ. He is the source of perseverance.

The Steps to Perseverance (vv. 2-6)

Now once the Lord Jesus Christ is recognized as the source of strength, the question might be asked, "How do I avail myself of that strength?" What are the steps to perseverance? Let me suggest four things.

Proper Doctrine (v. 2)

One sure way to be strengthened in grace is to transmit to others the truths which have embedded themselves in one's own heart. At the end of his life, the Apostle Paul was aware of a sufficiently fixed body of truth. That body of truth Paul had passed on to Timothy. Many people had witnessed this happening. Timothy must be persuaded of that truth so much that he himself would pass it on to other faithful men and then those faithful men would teach others also.

What you have here is a picture of the Christian faith persevering from generation to generation. It began with Paul's generation, then was passed on to Timothy's generation, then was passed on to the next generation, who would pass it on to the next generation. What would keep generation after generation going was the truth. And therefore, the truth must be passed on. The first step to perseverance is a conviction about the truth of the Word of God, a proper doctrine.

The Value of Perseverance

Proper Desires (vv. 3-4)

Now immediately when we start to form a conviction about the Word of God, there is something that the devil uses to choke out that conviction. The thing that the devil uses to choke out the Bible is the cares of this world, the deceitfulness of riches (Matthew 13:22). Therefore, at the very moment you become convicted of the Word, you must also determine that you will endure hardness. You will do without the things of this world, because the things of this world can easily choke out the Word. You must view yourself as one who has entered the boot camp of Jesus Christ.

> This is the army, Mr. Jones
> No private rooms or telephones
> You've had your breakfast in bed before,
> But you won't have it there anymore.
>
> This is the army, Mr. Green
> We like the barracks nice and clean
> You've had a house mate to clean your floor,
> But she won't help you out anymore.
>
> Do what the buglers command
> They're in the army and not in a band
>
> This is the army, Mr. Brown
> You and your baby went to town
> She had you worried, but this is war
> And she won't worry you anymore.

You are no longer a civilian, and therefore you cannot be concerned with civilian affairs. You are in the army of the Lord. And to be successful in the army, you have to have a desire to please your commanding officer. In boot camp, that drill sergeant becomes your life. Your desires must completely change. You cannot be concerned about yourself and your own social agenda. You must be concerned about pleasing that commanding officer. Jesus Christ is your commanding officer, and the proper desire is one of pleasing Him.

Proper Discipline (v. 5)

Paul here moves from the analogy of a soldier to the analogy of an athlete. When one entered the Olympic Games, he had to play by the rules. And the rules extended not only to the game itself, but to the training as well. Athletes, before they entered the games, had to swear with an oath they had fulfilled ten months of training. And no athlete was permitted to run unless he had played by those rules. So obviously, if you were not permitted to run, there was no chance of obtaining the prize. No one stood a chance of winning unless he played by the rules.

This implies that Christians need to be disciplined people who play by God's rules. So often we feel that we can cut a little here and compromise a little bit there, and then we begin slowly to lose the self-discipline of Christian living. No one perseveres in the faith the way he should unless he has discipline to play by the rules.

The Value of Perseverance

Proper Dependability (v. 6)

From the soldier to the athlete, Paul now moves to the farmer and the word translated "laboureth" is the Greek term *kopiao*, meaning "diligent toil." The reference is to a hardworking farmer. When a farmer plants a crop, he does not eat of it immediately. He must work hard throughout the entire season, and it is only after he has worked hard the entire season that he eats of the fruit. But he will certainly do so before the slothful farmer. The point is that a hard-working man has rights which the lazy man has forfeited.

So a person cannot figure this is taking too long. I am going off and doing something else. No, he must have dependability. He must stay with it for the long haul, and it is only then that he will be rewarded.

It is interesting to compare these three illustrations of the soldier, the athlete, and the farmer to the three temptations of Jesus. In the first temptation, Jesus was tempted concerning desires. Did He love bread or did He love pleasing God? In the second temptation, Jesus was tested concerning playing by the rules. Would He be the meek and lowly One or would he flamboyantly throw Himself off the tower? In the third temptation, Jesus was tempted concerning dependability. Would He seek to take the kingdom quickly as offered by Satan, or would He have the patience to wait for the Father's timing? In each instance concerning desires, concerning discipline, and concerning dependability, Jesus passed the test because He had the right doctrine. He always answered, "It is written." Jesus took the right steps toward perseverance.

The Standard of Perseverance (vv. 7-13)

Now concerning the source of perseverance and the steps to perseverance, Timothy must give some thought. He must grasp the meaning of what the Apostle Paul has been saying. The Christian minister needs understanding from the Lord in matters of self-discipline and approach to material matters. The minister must understand what he is headed for.

As he contemplates what is expected of him, let him remember Jesus Christ. Here is the ultimate standard of perseverance. This one of the seed of David went all the way to the cross of Calvary. The reason that God raised Him from the dead was because He finished the work that God had given Him to do. If Jesus had not finished that work, you and I would have no Gospel to preach. The reason I can call the Gospel "my gospel" is because of the perseverance of Christ.

This Gospel sometimes causes me to suffer persecution. Paul was treated like a common criminal and placed in prison because of his work in the Gospel. But even though Paul was bound, the Gospel never is. Christ persevered and went to the cross so that we might have the Gospel. Paul suffered in prison because of the Gospel, and Paul's hope is that you and I would do the same thing. As God's people, we have been elected to receive eternal glory. Just as Jesus was raised from the dead to a state of glory, because we are in Christ Jesus, we too have been

The Value of Perseverance

elected to eternal glory. We will obtain the consummation of our salvation. That being the case, let us persevere.

The Christians in Paul's day had a hymn that they would sing at baptism. The hymn went like this: If we be dead with Him, we shall also live with Him. This is the context of baptism (Romans 6:8). Baptism is identifying oneself with Christ's death, and if you have made Christ's death your own, Christ's life shall be your own also. This is what baptism pictures. To be baptized in Paul's day sometimes was tantamount to physical death (cf. I Corinthians 15:29-32). Why would people submit to baptism and put their necks on the line? They believed in an afterlife. They believed that if they entered into Christ's death, they would share Christ's life. That is why they endured suffering. They believed they were going to reign with Him. To reject Christ is to have Christ reject you. If a person does not place His faith in Christ, Christ is not going to change His Word and accept that person anyway. Christ will be faithful to His Word both concerning whom He will save and those He will damn. To do otherwise, Christ would have to deny Himself.

The point is that Christ is the standard for perseverance. He died and suffered in order that we might have the Gospel and glory. For us to avoid the life of Christ because we don't want the suffering of Christ is to miss the glory of Christ. On the other hand, to embrace the suffering of Christ in order to receive the life of Christ is to gain the glory of Christ. Christ received glory and life because He first was willing to go through suffering, and we must emulate that standard.

The Seriousness of Perseverance (vv. 14-26)

This matter of embracing the suffering of Christ to have the life and the glory of Christ is no trivial matter. Timothy is to charge men concerning these matters, and he is to charge them in the presence of the Lord, adding solemnity to the charge. This matter of embracing Christ or denying Him is the thing with which a pastor is to be concerned.

He is not to get involved in word battles that are useless. In other words, he is not to be involved in things that are trivial. All this kind of quibbling does is subvert the hearers. The word here translated "subverting" literally means "to turn upside down." The job of the pastor is to build up, not to turn upside down. Therefore, he must remember the main message.

It is, however, one thing to charge others; it is quite another to take oneself in hand. Timothy cannot charge others at the expense of his own life. Self-neglect is always a possibility, and the value of self-discipline cannot be overemphasized. The most effective refutation of error is a teacher who is the living embodiment of truth, a teacher with God's approval. Therefore, the teacher must live right, but that is not an easy task. The word translated "study" carries with it the idea of persistent zeal. Timothy must do his utmost to present himself as one approved by God.

Perhaps you have done a work that you were embarrassed to present. Most workmen feel ashamed when their product is shoddy and incompetent. How much

The Value of Perseverance   181

more should the Christian minister feel that way? A
Christian minister should be able to present his work
unblushingly before God for approval. He will be able
to do this when he is rightly able to divide the word
of truth. Literally, that phrase means "to cut a straight
road." Here it refers to the road of truth. In other words,
the pastor must be scrupulously straightforward in the
way he handles the Bible. He cannot use the crooked
methods which characterize false teachers. He must cut
the Word of God straight. This means men may disap-
prove of him, as they did with Paul. (v. 9), but such a
tactic always merits the approval of God.

Thus, the pastor is to stay away from godless chat-
ter. When pulpit time is comprised of empty talk rather
than the straight-forward presentation of the Word, ungodliness increases and false doctrine begins to spread
like gangrene. The doctrine and the morality of a church
slide when the Bible is neglected.

Yet people still err from the truth. They teach what
they think rather than what God's Word says. For example, in Paul's day Hymenaeus and Philetus taught the
resurrection was already past. They taught that the resurrection was a spiritual experience rather than a future
bodily fact. In so doing, these men missed the mark of
truth, and in addition, they overthrew the faith of some.
To have Christianity without a resurrection is to have
no Christianity at all. The resurrection is a basic element of the Christian faith.

This is why you and I need to stand firm on the
truth of God's Word. God's Word is a sure foundation

on which the Church rests. Buildings in Paul's day had inscriptions, and these inscriptions would state the purpose of the building. God has placed two inscriptions on His spiritual building, the church.

The first inscription is this: The Lord knoweth them that are His. The quotation comes from Numbers 16:5 from the account of Korah's revolt. The people of Moses' day were reminded that the Lord is able to differentiate between the true and the false. When unworthy elements sneak into the church, we are encouraged to know that God knows who are genuine and who are false. God unerringly knows His true children.

The second inscription is this: Let everyone who names the name of the Lord depart from iniquity. If the first quote referred to Godward justification; the second refers to manward justification. God knows those who are His, and we anticipate that those who are God's will depart from sin. The implication is that Hymaneaus and Philetus, by refusing to depart from sin, revealed that they were not God's true children.

From a discussion of the house, Paul now moves to a discussion about the contents of the house. In a house there are vessels not only of gold and silver, but also of wood and clay. Some vessels serve honorable purposes; others serve dishonorable purposes. My job is to make sure that I help the church, not hinder it.

Therefore, I have to purge myself from false teachers like Hymaneaus and Philetus. I have to take strong action against men like that. The only other time this word *purge* is used in the New Testament is in I Corin-

The Value of Perseverance 183

thians 5:7 where it is used of cleaning out the leaven in the church by excommunicating the sinner.

We must make sure that as vessels in the Lord's house we are serving an honorable purpose. We must be set apart exclusively to the work of God. We must be fit to be used by the Master, and we must be prepared to do any work that God calls us to do. We must be an honorable vessel.

We must flee youthful lusts. In the context, this is not so much talking about sex sins as it is impatience, love of dispute, novelties and ambition. Rather than getting sucked into all that, we need to follow righteousness, faith, charity, peace. But notice the peace is to them that call on the Lord out of a pure heart. Peace at the expense of purity is no peace. So the peace goes to those who are calling on the Lord, but men like Hymaneaus and Philetus must be purged.

Concerning these type of men, don't even get into a debate. The word *avoid* means more than evasiveness. Because these type of debates do nothing but breed quarrels, the only sane approach is to refuse to have anything to do with them. God's servants must not be characterized by arguing. Just as the Servant of Jehovah in the book of Isaiah opened not His mouth, so modern day servants of God must not strive. We should be kind unto all men and patient with those who oppose us. But this doesn't mean we ignore speaking the truth. We are always ready to teach these men the truth, but we must do so in a spirit of meekness. We must try to win our opponents, not antagonize them.

It may be that through indoctrination of the truth, God will change their minds and they will acknowledge the truth as truth. Right now, however, they have a two-fold problem. First, they need to recover, which literally means "to return to soberness." The devil has intoxicated their mind. Their conscience is numb. Their senses are confused. Their will is paralyzed.

But not only are they spiritually intoxicated; they are also snared by the devil. Their state is one of being intoxicated and captivated. The word translated "captive" literally means "to take alive." It occurs elsewhere only in Luke 5:10 where Jesus promised Peter that he would catch men. Well, Satan has caught some men alive as well and they need to be rescued.

Here is why the need for perseverance is so great. Our salvation and the salvation of others depends on it. Let us never forget that.

CHAPTER TWENTY-TWO

The Value of Peril

II Timothy 3:1-17

As we have moved through the book of II Timothy, we have discovered some very valuable gems. These items, even at first glance, are valuable things. The issue in chapter three, however, may not at first glance appear to be valuable, but indeed it is. We are going to discuss the value of peril.

In this passage, Timothy must constantly realize that perilous seasons will come, and he must constantly turn away from the kind of people who will make these seasons so grievous. Once this connection is seen, it is clearly understood that the phrase "the last days" is not to be limited to that period of time that immediately precedes the Lord's second coming. It would have been senseless to tell Timothy to avoid people who were not going to bother him at all. John states that as early as AD 90 it was the last time (I John 2:18). Peter says that Jesus was manifested in the last times or last days for us (I Peter 1:20). So, we know from Scripture that the last days or the last times in the Bible refer to that period of time ushered in by Christ's appearance on earth. It refers to the current dispensation that we are in. So, Paul is telling Timothy that he must realize that these last days — these days in which we are currently living — will be perilous times. This age will be characterized by ever-increasing wickedness.

The word *perilous* means "grievous, hard to endure, painful." These seasons then are areas of duress for the true church, difficult periods of time. Now why would God ordain for His church to go through these difficult time periods? What value would there be in peril?

Peril substantiates the validity of God's Word (vv. 1-5a)

What makes this time period so perilous is the people. It is the members of the human race living during that time who will cause all the grief. What's wrong with the people?

Well, for starters, they have misplaced affection. The Bible says that they will be lovers of their own selves. It is amazing that now entire sections of Christian bookstores are devoted to self-esteem and self-love. Some say that man's number one problem is that he does not love himself enough. Just the opposite is true. Man's number one problem is that he loves himself too much. What makes these days so perilous is that men have become lovers of their own selves.

Loving yourself too much naturally leads to loving money too much. Literally, the Greek reads here "lovers of self, lovers of silver." The number one goal of many people is that of making as much money as they can. Ethics are tossed aside and God is tossed aside in the pursuit of materialism. Men have become covetous.

Accumulating a bunch of things naturally leads to bragging. This word translated "boastful" was used orig-

The Value of Peril

inally of a man who wandered about the countryside peddling medicine, bragging about its healing virtue. Men today believe that the wealth they have accumulated is what makes them complete and whole individuals. To brag about the healing powers of riches is to reveal that you are a spiritual quack.

If the word *boasters* refers to people who swagger all over bragging, the word *proud* refers to people who are lifted up with haughtiness. As they brag about all they have been able to accomplish, they become overbearing. They become uppish.

And once a person is elevated with that kind of pride, he speaks disdainfully of others. The word *blasphemer* literally means "one who speaks against", that is, one who insults. It refers to people who insult God and to people who insult men. When they speak, their intent is to hurt and injure. They use scornful language.

This attitude of disdain even extends to their own parents. They lack submissiveness, and obviously this stems from an unthankful heart. They are not appreciative of the many acts of kindness which their parents have bestowed upon them. They are the recipients of common grace, but they lack common gratitude.

This even extends to that which is sacred. Holy things, established sanctities, are not regarded. They are completely impious, unholy. There is simply a lack of feeling among these people. They are unsympathetic to the things of home and the things of God. They are heartless. They lack the natural affection that people should possess.

This callousness extends to everyone they come in contact with. They are always in a feud with someone. They refuse to be reconciled. They refuse to ever enter into a truce. Rather, they prefer to hurl false and hostile accusations at each other. They are incontinent, meaning they are unable to restrain themselves. They are uninhibited, thoroughly lacking self-control. Rather, they are untamed, savage-like people; they are fierce.

Anybody or anything that is good receives their venom. Just like Judas, they would sell out Jesus Himself for thirty pieces of silver; they are traitors, and there is no stopping these people. They plunge full steam ahead in their deeds of violence. You can't reason with them. They know it all; they are blinded by conceit. Their minds are so high; they cannot lower themselves to take advice from anyone.

All of this blindness stems from a root spiritual cause. They love pleasure instead of loving God. Thus, the list ends the same way it began, by talking about affection. They love themselves, they love their silver, they love sensuality, but they do not love the Savior. There is the problem.

Now let us not think that these people exist only outside the church. No, these people many times keep a form of godliness, that is, an outward shell of religion. They maintain just enough church to maintain a cloak of respectability. There is a semblance of religion here. But even though there is a semblance of religion, we should not assume that these people are saved. Their lives clearly reveal that they have never known the saving power of

The Value of Peril   189

the Gospel. They are affiliated with the outward form of
Christianity, but they have never experienced its power
internally in their lives.

Now perhaps, this list causes someone to come to
your mind. This is not surprising. The Bible did tell us
that this age would be characterized by such people, and
every time we encounter the peril of such a person, the
Bible has been confirmed again. These people who try
to undermine the Bible actually help substantiate it, because every time they manifest their malice they help
this prophecy come true. Peril substantiates the validity
of God's Word.

Peril separates the vulgar from God's workers (vv. 5b-13)

The only response we can have to the people described in the first five verses is to turn away from them.
They cannot be reasoned with; they are not open to advice. Therefore, they have to be left alone. Now this may
seem harsh, but there is a reason for this ostracism as
the following verses make clear.

Out of the circle of these kind of men, from this sort
of people, come those who creep into houses. It is interesting that these men primarily focus on attacking
women. Isn't it interesting that this strange doctrine
is discussed when the man is not home? This goes all
the way back to the Garden of Eden when the serpent
talked to Eve when Adam was absent. Why do these
teachers try to get into houses through the women? Is

it because they know that women, especially this kind of woman, is easier to mislead? Is it because they reason that if we get the woman we get the rest of the family? I don't know, but the attack begins by seeking to captivate the woman. The Greek here is diminutive, the little woman. The King James translates it "silly women." The entire tactic reveals their attitude toward women in general. They see women as those who are fickle and can be easily duped. Women, according to them, are softies. They are easy marks. Women don't amount to much.

Notice the kind of women they go after. First, they go after a woman who has a sinful past. Here are women who are overwhelmed in their consciences. They have accumulated such an overwhelming amount of sin that they feel totally worthless. They are willing to grasp at any solution to get rid of this overriding guilt. They need their dignity restored.

But they are unwilling to repent. They still are under the control of various evil passions. They are still under the sway of evil impulses. Thus, the reason they want a teacher is not to learn the truth. Some women appear to be eager disciples. They appear to be taking it all in. They sit there with rapt attention admiring this teacher, but their unwillingness to confess and resist the evil promptings of their nature reveals that they are not interested in coming to the truth. They are merely interested in being under the tutelage of a man. As a counselor, you have to be wise to this. When people are not interested in taking the counsel, when they are ever learning but never able to come to the knowledge of the

The Value of Peril   191

truth, counseling should be discontinued because they are there for the wrong reason. A counselor that tolerates these kind of women and courts them is there for the wrong reason.

A hallmark of this kind of teacher is that he will denounce all other orthodox teachers and their ministries. When Moses went into Pharaoh and told Pharaoh to let the children of Israel go, Moses performed miracles by the power of God. Pharaoh's magicians, however, performed counter-miracles. Two of those magicians were named Jannes and Jambres. Their names mean "he who seduces" and "he who makes rebellious." Jannes and Jambres opposed Moses, and in opposing Moses, God's representative, they opposed the truth of God, because Moses was delivering the truth of God. The very minds that God had given them to receive the truth had become corrupted to the point where these men could no longer receive the faith. They deemed the faith be worthless and disapproved it.

The Bible is clear that these false teachers have a message that devours like a gangrene (II Timothy 2:16-17). Therefore, for a while it may appear that their purpose is going to be achieved, and the entire organism of the church will be destroyed. But the Bible's promise is that this will never happen. They shall proceed, but no further. Their folly, that is, their lack of understanding, their senselessness, will become eventually known to all. Just as Jannes and Jambres were revealed to be false, so the teachers of our day will be too.

God has a way of distinguishing in men's eyes between the true and the false. Timothy was able to see the truth. Timothy, when it came to pick a model, chose the Apostle Paul. It was clearly obvious that Paul was the type of teacher to emulate. Why?

First, his doctrine was commendable. Logically, this comes first. It was the teaching of the Gospel which first had impressed Timothy. But doctrine must be linked to life, and so the list of virtues now proceeds to bring out the practical character which stemmed from that doctrine. Paul's general manner of life and the apostle's chief aim in life were both worthy of emulation. His faith in God, his patience with respect to people, his love for even his enemies, and his steadfast endurance in trying circumstances all made Paul somebody worthy of copying.

Here was a man who had known incredible persecution and affliction. Timothy knew this. Antioch, Iconium, and Lystra were the very places Paul had visited on his first missionary journey. This was the journey where Timothy had met Paul and had been converted. Timothy had heard Paul's preaching at Lystra. No doubt he had seen the miraculous cure of the man who was born crippled. He had seen Paul restrain the multitude from worshipping him. He had seen Paul stoned. He knew the people thought Paul was dead. He had seen them drag Paul out of his native city. Timothy knew what kind of persecutions and afflictions Paul had gone through in those towns. Yet Timothy also knew that the Lord had delivered Paul out of all these trials.

If you are a Christian, if you claim to be joined to

The Value of Peril 193

Christ, then you are headed for a life of suffering. The life of Christ was a life of suffering. He was a man of sorrow and acquainted with grief. Therefore, if I am in Christ, I too will know a life of suffering. All those who desire to live godly in Christ Jesus will suffer persecution. Paul's experience was by no means peculiar. Scars are the price that believers pay for their loyalty to Christ.

The reason for the persecution is stated in verse thirteen. Evil men and seducers shall wax worse and worse. They are evil men because their attitudes, desires, words, and works are wicked. They are seducers because they are shrewd, crafty, deceitful individuals. They seek to deceive others, but in the process, they themselves are deceived. They think that they will gain a place of prominence by this deception, but as verse nine says, they will be reduced to nothing. Hence, in the process of deceiving others, they themselves are deceived.

In every age, there has been a man of God like Moses and deceptive religionists like Jannes and Jambres. The situation has not gotten any better; if anything, it has gotten worse. Evil men and seducers have waxed worse and worse. All this peril does, however, is make the men of God stand out in sharper relief. All the false teachers of Paul's day did was make his testimony all the more vivid. The peril of Paul's day sharply separated those who were vulgar from those who were authentically God's workers.

Peril solidifies the value of God's Word (vv. 14-17)

Against this backdrop of militant error, the Christian leader must stand firm on what he knows of the truth. He must be like a rock resisting the increasing fury of the waves. He is to continue to abide in the things which he has learned and has been assured of. The pastor is not merely to be a student of the Word. He must be completely assured of those things which he has studied. Learning is not enough. They are learning the Bible at liberal seminaries; but though they are learning it, they are not convinced of it. The Bible is not merely a book to be studied; it is a book to be studied in order that convictions might be formulated.

In contrast to these false teachers who were constantly advancing new and novel ideas, Timothy must be satisfied with that which he has already received. Two things will help with this satisfaction. Number one, look at the people who taught it to him. Paul taught it to him. Paul, as has already been stated, had nothing but pure motives. In addition to that, his grandmother and mother taught him the word of God since he was a little infant. Did they have deceptive motives? Hardly. The character of the people who embrace the Word of God says something about the character of the Word of God itself.

This brings up the second reason why Timothy must be satisfied with the Bible: not only because of the character of the people who taught him the Bible, but be-

The Value of Peril   195

cause of the character of the Bible itself. The Scriptures are holy. Remember in verse two, the perilous men were unholy. They had no regard for holy things. Timothy cannot be like that. He must venerate holy things, and if anything is holy, the Bible is holy. It is the Holy Bible.

Because it is the Holy Bible, it is able to make people wise unto salvation, but not merely if we approach it as an academic book. Remember it is not merely to be learned; there must be assurance concerning those things which we learn. In other words, the Bible is able to make a person wise unto salvation when it is appropriated through faith. Specifically, that faith is in Christ Jesus. The mere reading of Scripture is ineffective unless it is mixed with faith, and faith must be centered entirely in Jesus Christ.

The reason that Timothy should approach the Bible with such reverence, with such assurance, with such faith is that the Bible is a God-breathed book. All Scripture owes its origin and contents to the breath of God. The reason that the Bible is so profitable is because it is God-breathed. Thus, the Bible is the indispensable tool for profitable living.

The Bible is profitable to tell us what to believe. It is profitable for doctrine. Where should your doctrinal statement come from? It should come from the Bible. Here are two teachings; they are opposed to each other. Which one should I believe and which one should I reject? The Bible is profitable for doctrine.

But not only does the Bible tell me what to believe; it tells me how to behave. First, it tells me how to behave by rebuking wrong activity. It is profitable in the sense that it rebukes that which is wrong. But the Bible not only points out what is wrong; it is also restorative in character. It can correct the wrong. Some politicians can tell you what's wrong, but they can't tell you how to fix it. God's Word can tell you how to fix it. It is profitable for correction.

Then finally, the Word of God is profitable because once it corrects the problem, it can help you continue on that right path. It can provide the discipline necessary to continue on in the path of righteousness. It daily instructs me how to stay right and in that sense, it is highly profitable.

Thus, it is impossible to be a man of God without being also simultaneously a man of the Bible. If you want to be a man of God who is complete, completely completed for every good work, you need a Bible. The value of peril is that it drives us back to the Word. Here are all these competing fads and fashions. The temptation is great to give in. Where is my stability found (v. 14)? In what should I place my faith (v. 15)? What will actually be for my profit (v.16)? What can make me thoroughly equipped (v.17)? The answer to all these questions is the Bible. Peril solidifies the Bible's value.

CHAPTER TWENTY-THREE

The Value of Preaching

II Timothy 4:1-5

The background between II Timothy 3 and II Timothy 4 is the same; both chapters talk about the pastor's response to opposition. But though these chapters have that similar background, there is a discernible difference. Chapter 3 suggested that when Timothy is faced with opposition, he continue to abide in true doctrine. Chapter 4, however, takes it a step further. The pastor is not only a man who is to abide in sound doctrine; he is a man who must proclaim it. It is not enough to believe the truth. The truth must be boldly proclaimed even in the face of opposition. This brings us to the value of preaching.

The Mandate to Preach (v. 2a)

In verse two, Timothy is given five brisk commands. But the other four commands stem from and simply tell Timothy how to do this first command. Clearly, this imperative is the basis for the other four. Timothy is to preach the word. The verb *preach* is aorist tense. It appears that Timothy was at a crossroad in his ministry, a crossroad which demanded from him a definite resolution. Timothy had to make a once-for-all decision that would affect the rest of his ministry and Paul charges that this decision be one of preaching the word.

Now two things are involved here. First, the content

197

of the sermon. It must be comprised of the word. The pastor is not to preach his own ideas. The pastor is to bring God's message, not his own. Of course, this means that careful analysis of the text must be given. The pastor is not there to proclaim any other word that may exist out there. He is to proclaim God's word, the word. The word must comprise the content of the preaching.

But also in this injunction we see something about the delivery of God's Word. It is to be preached. It is to be proclaimed. It is to be heralded. What do we mean by this term *preaching*? It is sad that in our day the term *preaching* has come to denote "the delivery of a moral or religious discourse of any kind in any way." This is not what the Bible means when it uses the term *preaching*. The word *preaching* carries with it the idea of bold, public proclamation (cf. Matthew 10:27). The pastor is to be a man who is characterized by authoritative, open, forceful declaration.

Let's look at some examples of some men the Bible calls preachers. The first is Noah. The Bible calls Noah a preacher of righteousness (II Peter 2:5). Now in what sense was Noah a preacher of righteousness? Noah was a man who was empowered by the Spirit of Christ to preach to disobedient people (I Peter 3:18-20). While Noah was preparing that ark, he was also preaching. He was boldly and publicly warning the people of the impending judgment of God. When those people died and went to Hades, they knew the truth, because Noah had told it to them. Noah was a preacher.

The Bible calls Jonah a preacher (Matthew 12:41).

The Value of Preaching   199

The Bible calls that thing which Jonah did in Nineveh preaching. What did Jonah do in Nineveh? Jonah came into that city and boldly told the people that their sin merited the judgment of God (Jonah 3:4). Because Jonah boldly and publicly attacked their sin, because he preached, the people of Nineveh repented.

The Bible calls John the Baptist a preacher (Matthew 3:1-2). The Bible calls that thing which John the Baptist did preaching. What John did was publicly in the wilderness of Judea boldly attack sin and call for the people to repent of that sin. This bold, public declaration of the truth is called preaching.

So the point is that as far as content, the pastor should be exegeting the Scriptures, but as far as delivery is concerned, he is to use those Scriptures to boldly and publicly proclaim the truth of God. So genuine preaching is lively, not dry. Genuine preaching is timely, not stale. It is the earnest proclamation of the news of God. Especially to a man who in his natural temperament was timid, like Timothy, this mandate is very important. He must conclusively once for all decide that his ministry will be one of preaching the word.

The Motivation to Preach (v. 1)

Now obviously, when a man decides that his ministry will be characterized by a bold, public proclamation of the Word of God, he must find some motivation for that task. The task will not always be a pleasant one. The temptation will become great to alter the message or to tone down the delivery. Therefore, the pastor must constantly motivate himself to continue to preach the Word. Where does the motivation come from? Let me suggest two things.

The Ministers Who Have Preceded Him (v. 1a)

The Apostle Paul begins verse one by stating, "I charge thee therefore." We know, according to verse six, that the Apostle Paul was about to die. The aged warrior is about to pass on departing instructions to his younger, rather timid lieutenant. Paul was giving Timothy a charge to preach the Word.

I organized an ordination once and asked a pastor to give a charge to the church. And he asked, "How much do you want me to charge it? Is $19.95 enough?" Historically, at ordinations, we have referred to the messages as charges. This is when the seasoned pastors give instructions to the newer men entering the ministry. I still remember the 8th day of May, 1987 as I sat on the second pew of the Fellowship Baptist Church of Mansfield, Ohio and was ordained to Gospel ministry. I can remember the seasoned veterans of my hometown coming out and charging me to preach the Word. Here is motivation.

A charge to keep I have
A God to glorify;
A never dying soul to save,
And fit it for the sky.

To serve the present age,
My calling to fulfill,

The Value of Preaching

O may it all my powers engage
To do my Master's will.

Arm me with jealous care,
As in Thy sight to live;
And O Thy servant, Lord, prepare
A strict account to give.

I am motivated to preach the Word when I think of all the ministers who have preceded me who have charged me to do that very thing. A charge to keep I have.

The Master Who Will Appraise Him (v. 1b)

As high and as elevated as the charge at ordination, there is a still deeper motivation. That is, one day I will stand before God, and the Lord Jesus Christ will judge this ministry. In a sense, even now, His approaching footsteps can be heard. He is on the way and one thing is certain: He is coming to make determinations. He is coming to make judgments.

Some will still be living on this earth when He comes. Others will have already died. But whether I am among the dead in Christ or among those which are alive and remain unto the coming of the Lord, this ministry of mine will be judged by Christ.

There is no more certain thing than the fact that Jesus is coming again. Jesus will appear before my very eyes, and when He does appear, He will appear as King. He is not coming the second time as a meek servant. He is coming the second time as a sovereign king. My eyes shall behold the King. If that is not a motivation to remain true to the charge, I don't know what is.

> I shall see the King in His beauty,
> Shining forth in brilliant light.
> I shall start the praise of eternity
> When I see that glorious sight.
>
> Though each foe from hell fights for mastery,
> Though each sin of earth tries to conquer me,
> With one word my King shall claim victory
> When my eyes behold the King.

There is no greater motivation than that. What keeps a man faithful? Your opinion of me, says Paul, matters very little when compared with the estimation of God (I Corinthians 4:1-5). The Lord is coming, and He is the only One who can evaluate properly. We can't even evaluate ourselves properly. The estimation that matters is rendered by God, and He is coming to render that estimation. This is the motivation to preach.

The Methodology of Preaching (v. 2b)

As the preacher sets out with proper motivation to fulfill the mandate of preaching the word, how should he do it? What methodology should he employ? Let me suggest five things.

Be Persistent (v. 2ba)

Paul says that the preacher should be instant in season and out of season. That is, sometimes hard preach-

The Value of Preaching

ing will be popular and men will embrace it; it will be the season for preaching. At other times, however, it will not be the popular thing; preaching will be out of season. But it does not matter whether it is in season or out of season, we must always be prepared to do it. Easton paraphrases it this way: Be at your task whether men will listen or not. There is never a time in the pulpit ministry of a pastor when preaching is not the thing to do. It is always the thing to do. The pastor must always be at it regardless of the response. He must be persistent.

Be Penetrating (v. 2bb)

The word *reprove* translates the same word used of the Holy Spirit in John 16:8. The Holy Spirit is the One who reproves, who convinces, who convicts. The preacher who preaches in the power of the Holy Spirit will be a convicting preacher. His sermons will penetrate the shell and nail the heart. To go to church week after week and never be convicted is an exercise in futility. It is the pastor's job to convict, and if he produces no conviction, he is not doing his job. The sermon by its very nature is to produce conviction.

Be Protesting (v. 2bc)

Did you hear about the little girl who went to church, and when she came home, her mother asked her, "What did the preacher preach about?" The little girl responded, "Sin." The mother asked, "Was he for it or against it?" The little girl said she couldn't figure that part out.

It is sad to say, but it is difficult these days to discover what pastors are against. Rebuking has become very outdated. Isn't it a tragedy that Protestants don't protest anything anymore? Sin must never be toned down in the pulpit ministry of a pastor. His job is to rebuke, and if he is not rebuking, he is not Biblical. The moral status of many churches is weakened because the preacher is not rebuking sin.

Be Personal (v. 2bd)

The word here translated "exhort" is once again a word used of the Holy Spirit. It is the word *parakaleo*, one called alongside to help. In other words, the pastor is not to preach in vague abstract concepts. He is to be very practical and personal. He is to bring the truth of God alongside the congregant in order to help him. The word of God is to be applied personally to life situations in order that practical benefit may be derived.

There is a common statement that is coming now from many neo-evangelical churches. The statement is this: My pastor just preaches the Bible. Now for starters, let me say that fundamentalists are not preaching from the Koran. Why then would neo-evangelicals glowingly report that they only preach from the Bible to us as if we preached from something different? As I have ana- lyzed that statement, here is what I believe they mean. My pastor explains the Bible, but he does not apply the Bible. In other words, the pastor merely explains what the text says, but he does not tell the church member what to do with that text. The pastor leaves things in the

The Value of Preaching

realm of the abstract; he never applies and gets personal. If a pastor does that, he violates his commission. The pastor is to exhort people to specific styles of conduct. He is to be personal.

Be Patient (v. 2be)

Frequently, in the Bible God is said to be longsuffering. Here we see that the pastor is to adopt that God-like characteristic. As he persistently, penetratingly, protestingly, and personally proclaims the Word of God, he is to do so patiently. He is to patiently teach it over and over again. People don't get things the first time. Many times they don't get them the second time and the third time.

Teaching ministry always requires patience, and here is the balance. The pastor must be a profound hater of sin, but at the same time he must be a profound lover of people. We must be completely intolerant of the sin in people, but at the same time we must have a desire to work with the people entrapped in that sin. This requires patience.

The Malice against Preaching (vv. 3-4)

The reason why patience is necessary is given. There will come a time when men will not endure sound doctrine. I believe the closer we get to Christ's return, the worse this situation will become. The teaching of the Word of God can produce spiritual health. It can make people sound, but men will not endure it. Men will not tolerate it. Rather, they will be antagonistic to it and rebel against it.

When there is this kind of rebellion against the Word, Paul does not place the blame with the preacher. The problem is not the bold, public denunciation coming from the pulpit. In this case, the problem is not with the transmitter; it is with the receiver. The one who heralds the Bible is not at fault. The fault lays with the hearing of fickle men who make up the audience.

People want to have their ears tickled. People have their own perverted tastes and desires, and they will not give up until they find a teacher who is compatible with those perverted tastes and desires. Notice that Paul says they heap to themselves teachers. In other words, they pile up teacher after teacher until they find one that will accommodate their sin.

When a person is interested in finding a teacher that will vacillate, a teacher devoid of conviction, a teacher that will not reprimand, a teacher that will not apply, such a person is not interested in the truth. The demeanor of the minister has become more important than the content of the sermon. People become no longer interested in the truth itself, but in the style, oratory, the voice, the bearing, the looks, and the mannerisms of the messenger. When the truth to us is of secondary importance, we are on dangerous ground. Such a mindset means that we are susceptible to myths. The word used here of being turned unto fables was used by the Greeks of deviation from a true course. It suggests a wandering into counterfeits with no awareness that truth has been left behind. This is the danger of wanting a teacher (v. 3) but not a preacher (v. 2). So while it is true that

The Value of Preaching 207

good preaching teaches, it is also true that good teaching preaches. It is the malice toward preaching that is the lamentable state of the church today.

The Maturity of the Preacher (v. 5)

Now when the preaching of the pastor is attacked, he must respond with maturity. He cannot function like those who are against him. There is a great contrast between those described in verses 3-4 and Timothy himself in verse 5. When they exercise malice toward his preaching, Timothy is to respond with sobriety. The word *watch* translates the Greek word *nepho*. It means to be sober, to have a cool mind. When others respond negatively, Timothy is to be calm, steady, and sane. He is not to flip out at the fickleness of man.

When the man of God boldly proclaims the truth, he will be criticized and ostracized. There is no need flipping out about it; this is simply part of the ministry that must be endured. The way to respond is not by lashing out or getting depressed. The way to respond is with endurance that manifests itself in evangelism. If the message is so good, don't get bothered by people who won't listen. Go find somebody who will listen and preach the Gospel to them. Respond by doing the work of an evangelist.

The point is that no opposition should detract a minister from discharging his Gospel ministry to the full. Preaching the word, being instant in season and out of season, reproving, rebuking, exhorting are all things that must be constantly discharged. We cannot allow opposition to distract us from discharging them. Timothy has put his hand to the plough, and he must not look back until all has been fulfilled. He must maturely respond to the malice.

CHAPTER TWENTY-FOUR

Personal Inspection

II Timothy 4:6-8

You will notice in verse five that Paul tells Timothy to do some things. Paul said to Timothy, "But thou." You, Timothy, should watch in all things. You, Timothy, should endure afflictions. You, Timothy, should do the work of an evangelist. You, Timothy, should make full proof of your ministry. Paul said, "Timothy, there are some things that you ought to be doing."

But when Paul gets to verse six, he says, "For I." The reason that Paul was qualified to tell Timothy what to do is because Paul had taken care of himself first. I can tell you what to do because I have taken care of myself first. Similarly, Jesus said that before we try to straighten out other people, we need to straighten out our own lives first (Matthew 7:5). This is what Paul is saying here. "I can tell you what to do, Timothy, because I have taken care of myself first."

The Reasons for Self Inspection (v. 6)

In verse six, Paul gives us two reasons why we should inspect ourselves. Both of these reasons center around dying.

We have only one Life to Live (v. 6a)

Five years earlier, the Apostle Paul had talked about being offered (Philippians 2:17). This word *offered* was

209

used of drink offerings being poured on the altar. Paul talked about his life being poured out like a drink offering. Now, in II Timothy 4:6, he says that action is in the process of taking place. Paul's life is in the process of being poured out. Paul is in the process of dying.

The word that is translated "offering" is the Greek word *spendomai*; we get our word *spend* from it. When you go to the store and spend some money, you don't have the money any longer. When a drink offering is poured out, there is no way you can get all the liquid back in the cup. Once the offering is poured out, that is it.

We must realize that we have only one life to live for God. Once that life is over, that's it. It cannot be lived over again. Just as when you spill a glass of milk, you cannot get it all back into the cup. So, you cannot go back and start your life over again. Therefore, since we only have one life to live, we have to make sure that we live that one life right.

We can die at any time (v. 6b)

Paul says in verse six that the time of his departure is at hand. This word *departure* was used of ships being loosed from the dock. Paul was going to be loosed from this life and make his journey to heaven. Paul says that the journey from earth to heaven is at hand, that is, it could happen any moment.

Do you realize that what was true of the Apostle Paul is true of you and me? Our death could happen at any moment. We don't have to be ninety years old to die.

Personal Inspection 211

As I read the death notices each week, I notice babies that die, and young boys and girls that die, and teenagers that die, and young adults that die, and old adults that die. Death can happen at any point in life. We are always susceptible to death. The time of our departure is always at hand. All of us are only one heartbeat away from eternity.

So, there are two reasons why we should always be inspecting ourselves. The first is because we only have one life to live, and the second is we could die at any time.

The Method of Self Inspection (v. 7)

I know that because I only have one life, and because I could die at any moment, I need to inspect myself. Now the question comes, "How do I inspect myself?" I inspect myself by asking myself three questions.

Have I fought a good fight? (v. 7a)

Many times, as a child, I was in trouble for fighting on the playground. We have been taught that fighting is a bad thing. But here the Apostle Paul mentions a good fight. What would make a fight a good fight? There are two things.

First, a fight is a good fight when we fight the right person. Paul says in Ephesians 6:11-12 that we are not to be fighting against flesh and blood, but rather we are to be fighting against the devil. The Christian fight is between you and the devil. The Bible says that a fight is a good thing when we fight the right person, the devil.

Second, fighting is a good thing when we fight with power. In Ephesians 6:10, Paul says, "Be strong in the Lord and in the power of His might." For a fight to be a good fight, there has to be an adequate supply of power, an adequate supply of might. If two boxers get in the ring, and just lay on each other, that is not considered by boxing experts to be a good fight because there is no demonstration of might, no demonstration of power. And many of us are not fighting against the devil with God's power. Some of us are just not fighting a good fight.

Have I finished my course? (v. 7b)

I didn't ask you if you made mistakes in the course. We all make mistakes from time to time. But in spite of mistakes made, we should finish the course.

When I was in high school, I played the trumpet. There were several players in the band who could play the trumpet better than I could. One day the band director gave us a very difficult piece of music. He wanted the trumpets to play it. We made so many mistakes. One by one, trumpets would stop playing, but the band director never stopped us. He kept on directing. Because he was still directing, I kept on playing. Eventually, I was the only trumpet player playing that song in the entire band. It sounded awful, but I kept on playing. The band director, because I didn't quit, gave me a candy bar. Each one of those other trumpet players could have had a candy bar too, but they quit. God knows that you and I will make mistakes. But God wants us to hang in there and keep on playing. God wants us to finish the course.

Have I kept the faith? (v. 7c)

This phrase "keeping the faith" was used in Greek of keeping an appointment. If you promised the doctor that you would be at his office at 2:00, if you were there, you kept the faith. If you promised to help somebody at 4:00 and you were there, you kept the faith. Keeping the faith essentially meant that you were doing what you promised to do. People put their faith and trust in you, and you did not let them down. You did not betray that trust; you kept the faith.

Many of us have promised things to God. God, I'm going to live for you. God, you can depend on me. God, I will serve you. God, I will tell my mom and dad about Jesus. God, I will go to church. God, I will behave with my brothers and sisters. We make promises to God all the time. Have we kept the faith? Have we kept our appointment with God? Or have we let God down? Have we kept the faith?

The Results of Self Inspection (v. 8)

If we recognize that we only have one life to offer God and that we could die at any time, and if, because of that, we fight a good fight, finish the course, and keep the faith, what can we expect God to do for us? What are the results of self-inspection?

The result is the reward of God. When we are right with God and live the kind of life that God said we should live, we can expect to be rewarded. Why? Because the Lord is a righteous judge. God always does what is right. If we live right, God is morally obligated to reward that right living, because God does what is right. Paul at the time he wrote this was in jail. Nero, the emperor, was going to kill Paul because he was preaching the Gospel. Nero was going to hurt Paul because Paul did what was right. Paul never had to worry about God being unjust; God is a righteous judge. He rewards right living; He doesn't punish it like Nero did.

Now if Paul wanted to get out of jail and save his neck, he could stop living for God. Paul may have thought it was to his advantage to stop living for God. The fact of the matter is that sometimes in your neighborhood it appears to be to your advantage to not live for God. You don't want people laughing at you and making fun of you for bringing your Bible to school or praying before you eat, and so you just don't do what God says to do because you think it is to your advantage not to do so.

The problem with that thinking is that it is nearsighted. You are looking at the rewards of today rather than to the rewards of tomorrow. Paul's reward was not going to come from the hand of Nero; it was going to come later from the hands of God. It would come later.

This rewarding system is not only for Paul. It is for all those who love God's appearing. What does it mean to love God's appearing? It means to live right. A little boy's mother had to run to the store, and she told him not to get in the cookie jar while she was gone. As soon as the door closed, however, the little boy stuck his hand in the cookie jar. But his mother forgot her keys and she

Personal Inspection 215

came back in the door and there was his hand in the cookie jar. That boy loved his mother, but he did not love her appearing. Why? Because he was doing wrong. And if you are doing wrong when Jesus comes, you won't love His appearing. To love His appearing, you have to be doing right.

I need to live right because I have only one life to live and I could die at any moment. I live right by fighting a good fight, finishing the course, and keeping the faith. And if I live right, I can expect God to reward me for it, because God is a righteous judge who rewards all those who love His appearing.

CHAPTER TWENTY-FIVE

The Value of Your Presence

II Timothy 4:9-22

Twice in these verses the Apostle Paul admonishes Timothy to come and visit him. The Apostle Paul was soon to die. He and Timothy would not have much time to spend with one another. On top of all that, there had been a strong bond of friendship which had existed between Paul and Timothy. No one could take Timothy's place in the Apostle Paul's life. Hence we have the injunction for Timothy to come quickly.

Many times, I am convinced, we Christians give too little attention to how brief life really is, how little time we will have with our friends and loved ones on this earth. Moreover, I am equally convinced that many people do not recognize their presence as being valuable. To these people I would like to say with the Apostle Paul, "Do thy diligence to come shortly unto me." Your presence is valuable.

Your presence is valuable because some are defecting to the world (vv. 9-10a)

It is interesting that when Paul gives his first reason for Timothy coming, he lists the defection of Demas. Timothy is to come because "Demas has forsaken me having loved this present world." In this chapter Paul mentions two things that a person can love. He can love Christ's appearing (v. 8), or he can love this present

217

world (v. 10). In both verses the word *agapao* is used. In other words, you can sacrificially give because you are looking forward to Christ's return, or you can sacrificially give yourself to this world's system.

Let's see what the Bible has to say about love for this present world. The Bible tells us not to love the world (I John 2:15). The Bible even goes so far to say we cannot love God and the world at the same time. If you love the world, the love of the Father is not in you. To love the world is to cheat on God. It is spiritual adultery (James 4:4). When you become enamored with this world, and become consumed with accumulating riches, it can very easily choke the Word out in your life and make you unproductive (Matthew 13:22).

To function this way is to function with temporal goals in mind rather than eternal goals. The word translated "present world" is the Greek word *ainos* which refers to this world as an age. It denotes the world under an aspect of time. We can labor for that which is going to pass away with time or we can labor for that which will last for eternity. Demas chose to labor for the present rather than for the eternal.

When a person functions with only the temporal in mind, he does so not only to the detriment of himself, but he does so to the detriment of the church too. Notice that Paul said Demas hath forsaken me. To forsake the cause of Christ is to forsake other Christians as well. Paul clearly took Demas's defection personally. Demas had been a fellow laborer with Paul (Philemon 24), but now that was all forsaken. Demas had left his fellow la-

The Value of Your Presence   219

borer because of his love for this present world. In Paul's statement we feel his solidarity; we feel his sadness.

Those of us who have been saved for a while know the sting of defectors. We have seen our fair share of people leave the sphere of Christianity for this world's system. We have seen people depart from the cause of Christ, and it has grieved us. Because there are those who are defecting to the world, your presence and my presence is more important than it ever has been before. Your presence is valuable because some are defecting to the world.

Your presence is valuable because some are developing in the Word (vv. 10b-12)

People not only depart from our midst because they are defecting to the world. Some people depart out of our midst because they are developing in the Word. According to tradition, Crescens ministered in churches in Vienne and Mayence in Gaul, here called Galatia. Titus, of course, was a capable minister on the island of Crete. Now he has a new ministry in Dalmatia on the eastern shore of the Adriatic Sea.

Only Luke was left with the Apostle Paul. We should not suppose that Crescens and Titus had defected like Demas. No doubt they had left to pursue ministries to which God had called them. Probably the only reason Luke was detained was because Paul needed Luke's doctoring at this stage of his life. The others, however, were dispatched to ministries of their own.

When people leave our ranks to pursue ministries to which God has called them, there is a need for some people to step up and fill the jobs that have been vacated. There is a need to see new people get involved in ministry. So Paul admonishes Timothy to bring John Mark with him when he comes. Why? Because he would be profitable to Paul for ministry. Previously, you remember, John Mark had been a quitter. It was John Mark who was responsible for the breach that took place between Paul and Barnabus. But Paul, apparently, now feels that John Mark had learned some things. Now Paul feels that John Mark can be of benefit to him.

Paul had some great men who had been under his tutelage. Tychicus, for example, had always been a reliable associate. It was Tychicus who took the Ephesian letter to the Ephesians and the Colossian letter to the Colossians. Now Paul sends Tychicus to Ephesus to have a ministry of his own, but this means that Paul needs a new associate. Who better to fill that spot than John Mark?

It is not the job of the pastor to place many people permanently under his wing. It is his job to train ministers to go out and preach the Gospel in other places. But as these new ministers are called and sent, the home base must replenish itself. This is why your presence is so valuable. You can take the place of a Crescens, or a Titus, or Tychicus. You can be profitable to this ministry when others develop in the word enough to go out on their own.

Your presence is valuable because some are depending on your wealth (v. 13)

Another reason for Timothy coming is in order that he might bring a cloak that Paul had left at the house of Carpus when he was staying in the city of Troas. A cloak was an outer garment made of heavy material. It was circular in shape and had a hole in the middle through which one might place his head. It was winter time and Paul was getting cold in his dungeon. He needed this outer garment to keep him warm, and Timothy could bring it to him.

Paul not only wanted something for his body; he wanted something for his soul as well. Paul was a reader. Paul, wherever he went, loved to have books. In days of despair like these, nothing keeps the mind occupied and engaged like a good book. I believe you should teach your children to be readers. Nothing alleviates boredom, nothing makes a child exercise his mind and creativity like a good book. When you come, make sure you bring the books.

Then, and I believe above all else, Paul wanted something for his spirit. Bring the books, but above all, bring the parchments. Whatever these parchments were, they were books of some value. Vellum was too expensive to be used for common purposes. Only very special things were placed on parchment. Some have suggested that these parchments were Paul's legal papers, but I am more inclined to believe that these parchments were the Word of God. It is not impossible that Paul had valuable copies of the Scriptures, and what could be more encouraging in the hour of death than the Bible?

There is something that you can bring to your Christian brother. Maybe it is something material that will help him in his hour of need. Maybe it is something intellectual that will help in his hour of need. Maybe it is something spiritual that will help in his hour of need. But you have some wealth on which others are depending. Even if it is only to supply a Bible, you have helped someone immensely.

> This precious book I'd rather own
> Than all the golden gems
> That e'er in monarchs' coffers shone,
> Or on their diadems.
> And were the seas one chyrsolite,
> This earth a golden ball,
> And gems were all the stars of night,
> This book were worth them all.
>
> Ah, no, the soul ne'er found relief
> In glittering hoards of wealth;
> Gems dazzle not the eye of grief;
> Gold cannot purchase health.
> But here a blessed balm appears
> For every human woe,
> And they that seek this book in tears,
> Their tears shall cease to flow.

Your presence is valuable because some are deriding our witness (vv. 14-16)

When Paul thought of his Bible, this immediately

The Value of Your Presence 223

brought to mind his preaching ministry, a ministry of communicating the message of the Bible. But let us not think that Paul's preaching ministry was always well received. It was not. Alexander, the coppersmith, did Paul much evil when he withstood his words.

Paul mentioned Alexander in his first letter to Timothy (I Timothy 1:20). Alexander is one of the men who had shipwrecked the faith by insulting the Christian body of truth. His doctrinal deviations became so bad Paul had to excommunicate him. Perhaps there is no greater evil than the evil of attacking the Bible.

When people are characterized by doctrinal deviation, we need to be aware. When people attack the body of Christian truth, they not only attack the preacher, but attack the entire Christian community. Notice that Paul did not say Alexander attacked his words; he said Alexander attacked our words. The Bible is that body of truth on which we all rest, and for anyone to attack Christian doctrine is tantamount to an attack on all of us.

You would think, then, that many believers would rush to Paul's defense, but such was not the case. At his first trial, not a single man stood with him. Every person forsook Paul, but Paul was not bitter about that. He, in the spirit of Christ, prayed, "Father forgive them for they know not what they do." Paul asked that this crime might not be laid to their charge. This is vastly different from what Paul prayed for Alexander. He prayed that the Lord would reward Alexander according to his works. So in the case of his timid Christian friends, Paul prayed that they would not be punished. In the case of Alexander, Paul prayed that he would be punished.

So when it came to personal disappointment, Paul was ready and willing to forgive. When it came to an attack upon the Word of God, divine retribution was sought. Paul was not unduly enamored with people who hurt his feelings, but he was very troubled by people who were bent on sending others to hell by perverting the Scriptures. These people must be stopped. Paul quotes Scripture to support that position. He quotes Psalm 62:12 to show that God does reward every man according to his work. Therefore, Paul has a Scriptural basis for desiring Alexander to be stopped.

I am afraid that still today people are not zealous for the truth of God. When doctrinal deviates arise, many Christians are nowhere to be found. The time has come for more men to be like Paul and to stand up and be counted. Your presence is valuable because some are deriding our witness.

Your presence is valuable because some are delivered from wickedness (vv. 17-18)

The fact that Paul's friends deserted him is mentioned so that God's divine assistance might be brought into greater prominence. No one stood by me, but the Lord stood with me. The Greek *paristemi* means in other contexts "to stand by and help." Paul describes God's assistance as a strengthening. Even though no one was

The Value of Your Presence   225

there, God so strengthened Paul that he received great moral courage to proclaim the Gospel to his judges.

Throughout his entire missionary journeys, Paul had desired to preach the Gospel in Rome. He did not view his mission as complete until he was able to go to the capital of the empire and proclaim the truth of God. Now that goal has been fully accomplished. Paul now believes that all the Gentiles to whom he was sent have heard.

This never could have happened if God had not snatched him out of the jaws of death. Every time Paul was faced with danger, the Lord delivered Paul from that danger. Paul was confident that such protection would continue. Now this does not mean that Paul felt he was always going to be delivered from physical death, but it did mean that even if he did die, the enemy could never touch his soul. He would be preserved to see the heavenly kingdom of God. No human opposition or satanic opposition could keep that from happening.

This was a thought that Paul frequently contemplated in his writings. Nothing and no one can separate you from the love of God which is yours in Christ Jesus (Romans 8:3-5-39). Because this is true, look at what Paul says in Philippians 1:20. There is a boldness which comes to the Christian when he realizes that not even death can separate him from God. Even in your death you can glorify Him. That's what Paul does here. Even in the face of death, Paul could say, "To Him be glory forever and ever. Amen."

So, dear Christian friend, you will be delivered from

wickedness either through temporal protection or divine escort to the abode of heaven. Now if you come to grips with the fact that you will be delivered from wickedness even if you die, then you will have no fear standing up and being counted. Your presence will be seen as valuable when you recognize that you will always be delivered from wickedness.

Your presence is valuable because some delight in being welcomed (vv. 19-22)

Paul had often stayed in the household of Priscilla and Aquila. The same is true of Onesiphorus. Here were people that Paul had lodged with, eaten with, fellowshipped with. At the end of his life, he recalls the meals that he had with these people, the fun he had in their homes. There was a delight in his heart that he had been so favorably received by these people.

But not only had Paul been received for meals; he had also been received for ministry. Erastus went with Timothy to Macedonia, having been sent there by Paul. Trophimus was with Paul when he went to Miletus during the closing stages of his third missionary journey. Both of these men, Erastus and Trophimus, had been faithful helpers to Paul in the ministry. Paul reflects now upon their help with warm thoughts.

Then when we come to verse 21, we find some people that we don't know much about. Some traditions put Linus as a pastor in Rome. We have no idea whatsoever who Eubulus, and Pudens, and Claudia are, but

The Value of Your Presence 227

they were part of the brotherhood. That was enough. Some people have helped us out with meals. Other people have helped us out with ministry. Other people are simply our brothers. Simply because they are brothers, there is a warm affection here.

What creates this warm affection? Verse 22 gives us the answer. It is the Lord Jesus Christ. He is with your spirit, and He is with my spirit. That is what makes us one in spirit. In other letters, Paul would close by talking about the presence of the grace of the Lord, but here he talks about the presence of the Lord of grace. The presence of the Lord is what makes any meeting between any two Christians special.

Is it any wonder that Paul told Timothy to be diligent to come before winter? For a period of weeks, the Adriatic would be closed to shipping, and the Apostle Paul was anxious that Timothy reach Italy before transport delayed him. Paul was anxious to see Timothy. After all, Timothy was a brother. Timothy shared the spirit of Christ with the Apostle Paul. Just the delight of being welcomed by another Christian is worth you making an effort to be there.

> When trouble comes your soul to try,
> You love the friend who just stands by.
> Perhaps there's nothing he can do;
> The thing is strictly up to you,
> For there are troubles all your own,
> And paths the soul must tread alone;
> Times when love can't smooth the road,
> Nor friendship lift the heavy load.

But just to feel you have a friend,
Who will stand by until the end;
Whose sympathy through all endures,
Whose warm handclasp is always yours,
It helps somehow to pull you through
Although there's nothing he can do;
And so with fervent heart we cry,
"God bless the friend who just stands by."

CHAPTER TWENTY-SIX

An Introduction to Titus

Titus 1:1-4

The salutation in the book of Titus is much longer than that of either First or Second Timothy. This is in keeping with the nature of the book. Titus is a book which concentrates on the necessity of orderliness. In verse five, Titus was told to set in order the things that are lacking. So, order is very important to this epistle. It, therefore, stands to reason that even the salutation would be of an orderly nature.

The Fact of Paul's Apostleship (v. 1a)

On no other occasion does Paul describe himself as the servant of God. In Romans and Philippians, however, he does describe himself as the servant of Jesus Christ. The word translated "servant" is the Greek word *doulos*; it means "bond-slave." A man could only be the bondslave of one master. Thus, if Paul was a *doulos* of God and also a *doulos* of Jesus Christ, we must conclude that God and Jesus Christ are the same person. Jesus Christ is God.

It was Jesus Christ for whom Paul was an apostle. This title, "an apostle of Jesus Christ", was frequently used by Paul to draw attention to the official character of his service. Paul clearly sets forth at the beginning of each of his epistles the fact that he is God's apostle. Paul makes it plain that his apostleship was not of men, nei-

229

ther by man, but by Jesus Christ (Galatians 1:1). Paul was chosen and ordained of God to preach the Gospel and make known the good news that Jesus died to provide salvation for all. God had made Paul an apostle.

The Purpose of Paul's Apostleship (vv. 1b-3)

There were some specific reasons why God had chosen Paul to be an apostle. The first reason was for the purpose of furthering the faith of God's elect. There are only two other times in the Scriptures where Paul uses the phrase "God's elect." The first is Romans 8:33. In that context, God has predestinated all saved people to be conformed to the image of His Son (Romans 8:29). This is the election which Paul is talking about in verse 33. It is an election of saved people to glorification. The second time this phrase is used is in Colossians 3:12-17. Because we have been chosen and elected to a state of glorification, there is a necessity for working that out daily in our lives. God has chosen us to do the things described in verses 12-17.

The Apostle Paul now says that God has made him an apostle for the purpose of furthering the faith of God's elect. The phrase "the faith" refers to the body of Christian truth as contained in the Scriptures (cf. Jude 3). There is a body of Christian truth which was once delivered for the saints. That body of Christian truth, Jude refers to as "the faith." If God has elected His people to be the agents of His purpose, and has chosen them to specific realms of service, then they had better know what God's purpose is and what realms of service

An Introduction to Titus   231

are important. For that reason, there is a necessity for a body of truth to be delivered to God's chosen people. The Apostle Paul was ordained an apostle to further that body of truth. He was chosen as an apostle to write Scripture.

Paul was not only commanded to write Scripture, but he was also commissioned to help people recognize and understand Scripture. He was to help people acknowledge the truth. The word here translated "acknowledging" is the Greek word *epignosis*, and it carries with it the idea of recognition. Paul was to help people recognize the truth of God. God's servants are not to be ignorant of the field of truth.

But our recognition of Christian truth has a distinct and definite purpose, and that purpose is to lead us into godliness. As we have seen, God has elected us to lead godly lives. Therefore, Paul was to write Scripture and help people recognize it as Scripture for the purpose of them progressing in godliness.

This body of Christian truth which Paul had been commissioned to further was not only applicable to this present life (though it is applicable to this present life), but also written in hope of eternal life. The Greek preposition *epi* here translated "in" points to the fact that such hope is the basis on which the super-structure of Christian service is built. We serve God and engage in godliness because we have a definite future hope, a hope of eternal life.

Notice what this hope is based on. It is based on the promise of God. And God, Paul says, cannot lie. When we use the word *hope*, many times we are simply refer-ring to mere expectation and desire. We say, "I hope the Phillies win the pennant." Now that has no basis in fact; that is mere expectation and desire. When, however, the Bible uses the word *hope*, it is referring to a certain real-ity. Bible hope is based in the promises of God, and God cannot lie. God is free from falsehood, and therefore His promises in general, and His promise concerning eternal life in particular, is absolutely trustworthy.

So the promise remains sure and steadfast in spite of the fact that it was made even before the world began. Before times eternal God blue-printed a plan of salva-tion, but just because the promise is an old one doesn't mean that it is a forgotten one. As a matter of fact, it is still so fresh in the mind of God today that He is in these due times continuing to manifest His Word through preaching.

This word which is manifested through preaching must refer to the message of the Gospel which forms the content of Christian preaching. This Gospel was something that had been committed to Paul, that is, en-trusted to him. So, here we have the third purpose of Paul's apostleship. Not only had he been commissioned to write Scripture, and to help Christians recognize and apply Scripture, but here we see that Paul had been com-missioned to preach the Gospel. The Gospel had been committed unto Paul in order that he might preach it.

Every time that Paul wrote a pastor friend, he always stopped with wonder and amazement at the fact that God had called him to preach the Gospel (cf. I Timothy

An Introduction to Titus 233

1:11; II Timothy 1:10-11). Paul was amazed and wanted all his pastor friends to be amazed with the fact that God had called them to be preachers of the Gospel.

Paul makes it plain that this ministry was not something he assumed upon himself. It was assumed in response to a commandment of God our Saviour. Paul received his commission directly from the Lord, and this will be vitally important for Titus to understand as he undertakes the responsibility of ordaining elders. To be sure, he was to look for qualified men, but a prerequisite to godly qualifications is a divine call. That must come first.

The Recipient of Paul's Apostleship (v. 4)

Certainly, one of the biggest recipients of Paul's apostleship was this fellow by the name of Titus. Though we don't know a tremendous amount about Titus, we do know that Paul had led him to the Lord. He was Paul's own son after the common faith. There are only two other people in the Bible that Paul refers to as spiritual sons, and they are Timothy (1 Timothy 1:2) and Onesimus (Philemon 10).

Titus is not mentioned at all in the book of Acts, but he is mentioned in the book of Galatians and in the book of II Corinthians three times. It may be gathered from II Corinthians that Titus was selected for a particularly difficult and delicate mission, and since the outcome appears to have been a happy one, it is clear that Titus was a man of unusual tact who possessed high qualities of leadership. His allotted task in Crete certainly demanded much wisdom and strength of character, and the apostle's confidence in him accords completely with what is known of him elsewhere.

Thus, while the faith is a common or a universal faith (it is for everybody), Paul had a special vested interest in this pastor friend, Titus. He was Paul's spiritual son. It is important for us to understand that Paul can call Titus a son, but Titus cannot call Paul a father. This is not permitted. Jesus said in Matthew 23:9, "Call no man your father upon the earth." Paul could maintain a son relationship with Titus, but Titus could not maintain a father relationship with Paul. Titus only had one spiritual father, and that was his Heavenly Father.

Paul wished three things for his spiritual son and pastor friend. He wished him God's grace, God's mercy, and God's peace. Certainly when Titus accepted the Lord as His Saviour, he received grace, and mercy, and peace, but there is a necessity for these things to be continued in the life of a believer. There is a necessity for the multiplication of grace, mercy, and peace in the life of the believer.

But this grace, mercy, and peace is only available through God the Father and the Lord Jesus Christ. Notice that Paul refers to Jesus Christ in this verse as Saviour. This is interesting because in the previous verse he had referred to God as Saviour. Obviously, Paul regarded Jesus as God, and the Son and the Father as one.

Paul, the apostle, who was commissioned to write God's word, teach God's word, and proclaim God's Gospel, was writing to one of his converts who was now

An Introduction to Titus

a preacher instructing him in the ways of church orderliness and leadership training. This is the purpose of the book of Titus.

CHAPTER TWENTY-SEVEN

The Qualifications of a Pastor

Titus 1:5-9

After his formal salutation, Paul moves directly to Titus' specific commission. Paul had presumably visited Crete and left Titus there to carry on the work. Paul had departed from the island of Crete, perhaps hurriedly, and had instructed Titus to set in order the things that were wanting, the things that were left undone. No doubt Paul refers to some arrangements which he had begun but found it impossible to complete.

The Greek word translated "set in order" occurs nowhere else in all the New Testament. It means "to be proper, to make straight, to make right." It is used in the sense of setting right again what was defective. This commission issued to Titus was not necessarily to add to what the apostle himself had done, but to restore what had fallen in disorder since the apostle had left. There were many things left unfinished, which Titus was to set in order. Perhaps the most outstanding thing which needed to be done was the ordaining of elders in every city.

The church at Crete was in a disorganized state, and Titus had therefore two important duties. He had to complete what Paul had left incomplete, and he had to ordain elders. It is essential for Christian churches to possess some orderly scheme of government, and the apostle had previously impressed this on his close as-

237

sociates. In the phrase "as I had appointed thee", the "I" is emphatic, not to bring out Paul's egotism, but his authoritative endorsement of the elder-system.

The first thing we notice about the term *elder* is that it is used interchangeably in this passage with the word *bishop*. In verse 5, Paul tells Titus to ordain elders, and then in listing the qualifications, he states in verse 7 that a bishop must be blameless. So the term *elder* and the term *bishop* are words which refer to the same office. In I Peter 5:1-2, Peter tells the elders to feed the flock of God, and the term there translated "feed" is the same word translated "pastor" in Ephesians 4:11. So, elders are commanded to pastor the flock of God. Similarly, in Acts 20, Paul calls out the Ephesian elders (v. 17). In verse 28 of the same chapter, Paul tells the Ephesian elders that the Holy Ghost has made them overseers (the same word translated "bishop" in Titus 1:7). The Holy Ghost has made these elders bishops for the purpose of feeding the church of God, and once again the word translated "feed" is the same word translated "pastor" in Ephesians 4:11. So, the Holy Ghost has made these elders bishops for the purpose of pastoring the church of God.

It is not difficult to figure out that the New Testament uses the words *elder*, *bishop*, and *pastor* all interchangeably. The word *elder* refers to the maturity of the man in the faith. As you remember, Paul told Timothy that an elder was not to be a novice or a new convert. The term *bishop* refers to what this mature man is to do. He is to oversee. This is a fact that often gets neglected in churches. Some churches have the idea that the pastor is to preach, and that deacons are to oversee. This is not a Bible concept of church government. The elders are the ones whom God has tagged with the title "overseer." Then the term *pastor* refers to the motive with which the pastor is to oversee. He is to oversee with the heart of a shepherd. The nurturing of the flock should be his heart.

The Necessity of Ordination (v. 5)

The first thing Paul told Titus to do was to ordain elders. The word there translated "ordain" is the Greek word *kathistemi* which means "to cause to stand, to set." Thus, eldership is something that begins with the call of God. In Acts 20:28, Paul told the Ephesian elders, "the Holy Ghost has made you bishops to pastor the church of God." So, the first prerequisite to eldership is a divine call.

If a man is divinely called to be a pastor, he will pursue that calling. The word translated "desire" in I Timothy 3:1 is a word used of runners passing a baton in a race. In other words, pastoring is something that a man pursues. He reaches out his hand to grab the office based on the fact that God has called him. This is vastly different from the office of deacon. With regards to deaconing, the office sought the man (Acts 6:3). Look you out among you, the Bible says. No man should ever seek the office of deacon. If he does, he proves that he is not qualified to be a deacon. In the New Testament, as far as deaconing is concerned, the office seeks the man, but with regards to the pastor-elder-bishop, the man seeks the office in response to a divine call.

Suppose a man says, "God has called me to be a pastor." Should we automatically believe him? Or, is there some objective way whereby the church can verify that calling? There is a way the church can verify the calling, and that process is ordination. So, while it is true that eldership originates with a divine call, there is also the importance placed on that call being verified through the process of ordination (Acts 14:23).

So, there are three things that are stressed in the Scriptures with regard to eldership. The first is a divine call. The second is godly qualifications because God equips those whom He calls. The third is elder recognition. This calling and qualifications must be recognized by the church. Certainly, if the presbyters are the ones who lay on hands in the process of ordination, those presbyters should be ordained themselves (I Timothy 4:14).

So there is a fine line. If a man has been truly called of God, he should preach regardless. He should preach because God told him to. On the other hand, however, we have to recognize that not everyone who claims to be called of God is called of God. God, therefore, has given the church a way to distinguish the false professors from the true professors, and this is the process of ordination. I would encourage any man who is pursuing God's call to also pursue ordination. It will add tremendous credibility to his ministry.

The Qualifications of a Pastor

The Necessity of Qualifications (vv. 6-9)

The word *blameless* is an important word to Paul as far as church administration is concerned. In talking about elders in verse six, he states the necessity of them being blameless. When he switches terms to bishop in verse seven, he again states the necessity of the pastor being blameless. So, the pastor should be blameless as far as who he is, and he should be blameless as far as what he does. Both in his character and in his deportment he should be above board.

This same word is used in I Timothy 3:10 with reference to deacons. So, Paul in his writings very emphatically reflects the need for an irreproachable moral standard in all types of Christian office. I have heard some people say, "No man is blameless." Now this is not true or God wouldn't have made it a requirement. God is not asking for a man who is sinless, but he is asking for a man who is blameless.

Qualifications concerning his family (v. 6)

The first thing we see here is that the pastor is to be the husband of one wife, literally a "one-woman man." Certainly this doesn't mean that the pastor has to be married. If that is true, then Jesus wasn't qualified to be a pastor and neither was Paul. These qualifications in verse six are for those who do have families. If a man has a family, he is to be a one-woman man. That means several things. First, he cannot be guilty of bigamy. He cannot be married to more than one woman. This may not seem like a big deal to us Americans, but there are many missionaries who have accommodated this requirement in other cultures because they could not find a man who only had one wife. But the Bible says that has to be the case. Second, the man must not be divorced and remarried. Such a man is guilty of having two wives, and thus he is not a one-woman man. There is another point that is often missed on this score. The Greek also carries with it the idea that a pastor is not to be a ladies' man. He should be one totally dedicated to his wife. He should not be flirtatious.

The second family qualification mentioned here for the pastor concerns his children. He is to have faithful children meaning that his children are to be in the faith. His children are to be saved. If a pastor has children who have rejected Christianity and turned their backs on the faith, he is not qualified to be a pastor.

The qualification proceeds further. Even if the children are in the faith, they are not to accused of riot or unruly. The word translated "riot" is the Greek term *asotia* which literally means "an inability to save." It refers to those who waste money on their own pleasures. The word is used of the prodigal son who wasted his substance in riotous living. If a pastor has a son or a daughter who could be classified as a prodigal, he is not qualified to be a pastor.

Then, of course, the pastor's children should not be accused of insubordination. They should not be unruly. The home is to be regarded as the training ground for Christian leaders, and thus elders who have children are expected to have a Christian household.

Qualifications concerning his faculties (vv. 7-8)

When Paul tells us a second time that pastors are to be blameless, he mentions the reason why. They are to be blameless because they are the stewards of God. The metaphor pictures a manager of a household or estate. The pastor has to realize that he is managing God's house. Hence, the necessity of being blameless, not only with regards to his family, but also with regard to his faculties.

The pastor is not to be self-willed. The word is only used here in the New Testament. It means "self-complacent, assuming, arrogant." In other words, a pastor is not to be selfish or self-centered.

In addition, the pastor is not to be soon angry. He is not to be a hot head. The pastor cannot get angry at the least little thing that comes his way. He cannot fly off the handle or give people a piece of his mind. He must exercise love, compassion, humility, and sacrifice.

Next, the pastor should not be given to wine. Now certainly this is a prohibition against alcohol, a command to total abstinence, but the qualification here goes much beyond that. Persons who sit over wine and continue to drink, will become loud and boisterous. In many instances, arguments arise and sometimes lead to bodily injury. A pastor may not show that kind of spirit. He must be a peaceable man, not quarrelsome. The Greek construction not only prohibits wine, but it also prohibits acting as if you have had wine. So obviously, the pastor should not be a striker. He should never come to blows with anyone.

Then the pastor is not to be given to filthy lucre. He must not be desirous of base gain financially. Certainly, while the attitude of the congregation ought to be one of taking care of the preacher, the attitude of the preacher ought to be that he is not in it for the money. The phrase "filthy lucre" carries with it the idea of shameful gain. This admonition is against preachers who earn their paycheck dishonestly, preachers who take a paycheck without putting in the necessary time and energy. The admonition is not even against pastors desiring enough money to take care of their families. The admonition is against preachers who take a paycheck through dishonest means.

A pastor should also be a lover of hospitality. In the early church, special emphasis was placed on this duty. In those days it was absolutely necessary that homes be opened to those Christians who traveled. This was to be practiced habitually, by all believers, but especially by the pastors. Certainly, today we should be given to hospitality much more than we are.

A pastor should also be a lover of that which is good. The admonition is to love both good men and good things. If it is right and good, a pastor should be in favor of it.

He should also be sober, not only with reference to liquor, but also concerning other things. The word means "sober-minded, self-controlled, discreet." A pastor is to be sober in all walks of life and behavior.

Not only should he be sober, but he must also be just. He must be honest, upright, open and above board in all his dealings with his fellow man. He must be holy. The world watches the lives of all believers, especially the lives of pastors. It is of utmost importance that a pastor be careful to live above reproach. A leader in the church can do little good if he is not holy in his living.

Then a pastor must be temperate. He must be calm minded. The word here carries with it a more deliberate effort at self-control than does the word *sober*.

Qualifications concerning his faith (v. 9)

Further qualifications are demanded on the doctrinal side for the pastor. He must cleave to the faithful word. A pastor is to hold fast to pure doctrine. He is to definitely oppose all systems of false teaching. He must be a man who is firm in doctrine. He must be a man who can be relied upon and trusted concerning spiritual matters and depended upon to maintain and defend the pure gospel of the grace of God.

This can only be accomplished if the pastor has been taught himself. The statement "as he hath been taught" makes it quite clear that a pastor should be one who has been taught, not a novice, a learner, or a babe in Christ. He is to be well established in the Word of God. The pastor must have clear convictions and an understanding of the Bible.

Paul makes it plain that he must be prepared to cling to that truth even in the face of opposition. He must be able by sound doctrine both to exhort and convince the gainsayers. There is an authoritative and objective system of Christian doctrine contained in the Bible, and the pastor must cling to that regardless of circumstances or favorability.

The pastor is not only to denounce the gainsayers, but also convince them. He was not to compromise, but rather to persuade them, if at all possible, to turn from error and embrace the truth.

A good minister uses both exhortation and argumentation. Those who know the truth need to be exhorted and admonished concerning the truth, but those who are ignorant of the truth need both exhortation and argumentation. We should exhort them to turn to Christ and give them a sound argument as to why they should.

A gainsayer is a person who speaks against the truth. Now certainly we would hope that all those who speak against the truth are outside the church, but from time to time even church members can speak against that which is right and proper. The pastor must be prepared for such people and be so familiar with right doctrine that he can effectively exhort and communicate right Christian doctrine.

CHAPTER TWENTY-EIGHT

Dealing with Gainsayers

Titus 1:10-16

The Characteristics of Gainsayers (vv. 10-11)

In verse nine, Paul told Titus to ordain elders who could exhort and convince the gainsayers. Now he proceeds to describe these gainsayers. Apparently, these gainsayers were numerous in quantity, and Paul says in verse ten that they are characterized by three undesirable qualities.

First, they are unruly. The underlying Greek word is *anupotaktoi* and carries with it the idea of insubordination. These gainsayers rebelled against the official authority of the church. So, the first mark of a gainsayer is that of a cavalier spirit, an unwillingness to submit to church authority.

Second, they are empty headed in their teaching. They are vain talkers. The Greek word *mataiologoi* carries with it the idea of doing much talking, but saying nothing.

Then third, they are deceivers. Because they are deceived themselves, they consequently deceive others. They lead others astray.

Now while all such characteristics are dominant in all heresies, they were particularly evident among the Jewish teachers who were active in Crete. Titus should especially watch out for those of the circumcision. Paul knew Titus would receive much opposition from the legalizers and Judaizers, and therefore gave this warning.

Strong medicine is prescribed for these false teachers. Their mouths must be stopped. The word *epistomizo* was used of bridling horses or muzzling dogs. At all costs, these men were to be prevented from doing further damage. The word here is so strong that this is the only place it is found in the New Testament.

Certainly, one of the reasons that Paul felt this heresy must be dealt with so sharply is because of the effect it was having on the family. These heretics were turning whole families away from the truth. By affecting one or two members of a family, the false teachers were able to subvert or upset entire households. Presumably these families were Christian, and any movement which causes such rifts in family life must be carefully checked. Paul makes it plain that these rifts were not caused because these men were teaching the truth. On the contrary, these houses were subverted because the heretics were teaching things which they ought not.

Their motive for teaching error was financial. There was a strong mercenary element about them which merits the apostle's strong condemnation. For filthy lucre's sake they taught. This vividly brings out the sordid character of these empty religionists. Wherever mercenary considerations dominate a religious movement, the same strong condemnation is deserved. They taught doctrines that made them popular, drawing people to them, causing their followers to have confidence in them and contribute money to them instead of to their local church.

The Confirmation about the Gainsayers (vv. 12-13a)

The word used here for "prophet" was, in Paul's day, often applied also to a poet. The Greeks looked upon their poets as inspired men, believing that they wrote under inspiration of the gods. So, Paul supports his argument by appealing to a venerated Cretan critic who was himself a Cretan. The lines quoted here are from Epimenides, a sixth-century philosopher whom his countrymen had raised to mythical honors. Many ancient writers, including Aristotle and Cicero, mention him as a prophet, and Paul cites him by this well-known description. Because a well-known Cretan condemns his own people, Paul cannot be charged with censoriousness for his exposures.

It was very important for Titus to be careful in selecting persons for leadership in the churches on the island of Crete, for the people there were well known for their unwholesome character. The Cretans were known as being "always liars." The Cretans were notorious for untruthfulness and it is strikingly confirmed by the Greek language containing a word *cretizo* meaning "to lie."

But not only were the Cretans given to lying, they also had an unenviable reputation for the sensuous. The phrase "evil beasts" represents a maliciousness which is akin to the animal world, and the phrase "slow bellies" describes their uncontrolled greed as "idle gluttons." So, by the famous poet's own pen, the Cretans were described as being liars, savage, and gluttonous.

The Apostle Paul is about to urge Titus to take a strong hand with this unruly element in the church, but he begins by first priming him on the well-known characteristics of the people with whom he is dealing. This principle has constant relevance, for every minister of the Gospel must of necessity be cognizant of the character of his people, however distasteful the facts may be.

Paul under the inspiration of the Holy Spirit endorses the veracity of this proverbial saying. It may be through personal experience, or else by common report, that Paul knew the Cretans were a difficult people with whom to deal. Their own prophet had confirmed it.

The Command Concerning the Gainsayers (vv. 13b-16)

Paul's command to Titus is to *sharply* rebuke these false teachers. The word sharply means "cuttingly, severely." It comes from a word which means "to cut off." He was not to soft-pedal his message, nor be mealy-mouthed. He was to call sin by its right name. He was to spare neither their thoughts nor their feelings. They needed to be rebuked sharply.

Such severe reproach has a saving purpose, that they may be sound in the faith, a reference to the accepted body of Christian doctrine. We should always have this redemptive purpose in mind whenever we deal with those who are in error. The purpose is not to win the

Dealing with Gainsayers   251

argument or put the other person down as much as it is to make the erring one sound in Christian doctrine. Much vituperation would have been saved had Christians always had this saving purpose in mind when dealing with those erring from the faith.

There were two specific strands of heretical teaching in their doctrine that had to be dealt with. The first was Jewish fables. The fables referred to here were probably the idle superstitions and conceits of the Jewish Rabbis. The Jewish fables were no doubt akin to those mentioned in I Timothy 1:4 and probably consisted of useless speculations based on the Old Testament. The people were not to pay attention to a discourse of fiction or mystic ideas. The fables to which Paul refers were composed of frivolous, unfounded tales and stories which were regarded with high esteem and as of much importance. Some leaders desired to incorporate them into the doctrines of Christianity. Paul, having been reared among these superstitions, knew the fallacy of them and how they eventually drew the mind of the believer from truth, and would corrupt true religion.

One of the most successful schemes of the devil in damning souls has been to mingle fable with fact. There are many religions that preach some truth but God is not the author of confusion. Fables and fiction confuse the mind, but the truth of God makes sure the heart and mind and sets the sinner free.

The other strand which turns men from the truth is the commandments of men. This is strongly reminiscent of the heresy mentioned in the book of Colossians which also consisted of the commandments of men (Colossians 3:21-22). False teaching and false practice are usually close companions, and find willing allies in men occupied in turning others away from the truth.

There is a necessity then for Christians to keep themselves pure. Paul's injunction here is an echo of the words of Jesus in Luke 11:41. Paul also expounded this same idea in Romans 14:20. A pure mind cannot become contaminated by physical contact. Pure minds will have no relish in seeking unnecessary defilement.

"Unto the pure all things are pure" does not mean that dope and alcoholic beverages, which will dull the mind and destroy the body, are pure. There is a direct teaching here concerning the ceremonial meats and drinks among the Jews. Some foods were regarded as clean and could be eaten, while others were considered unclean and were therefore forbidden. What Paul is saying is that those distinctions ceased when Christ died and rose again.

In the Christian era, it is not what we eat or drink that saves us or damns us. In Paul's day, under the Law of Moses, a Jew dare not eat pork or drink certain drinks. But in this day, meats and drinks neither save nor damn, although a child of God, led by the Spirit of God, will not eat or drink those things that will destroy the body.

A person who is a true child of God will not use this passage to attempt to prove that all things are right and lawful for the Christian. There are those who say that if you think something is not sin, then to you it is not sin but such reasoning is not found in the Word of God.

Dealing with Gainsayers

The principle here involved is a pure, truly pious mind. If we have such a mind, we will not eat or drink those things that will destroy our testimony. The believing heart does not major on the distinction of food and drink, festivals, ceremonies, rites, holy days, holidays. These things have nothing to do with purity of heart and spirit, and the conscience of the believer is not to be burdened with nor enslaved by them.

No stronger condemnation of the would-be purifiers could be made than the assertion that there is nothing pure to those who are defiled and unbelieving. Those who are defiled can touch nothing without defiling it, hence to them nothing could be pure.

This statement is very clear. The unbeliever is lost, totally depraved, without strength, hopeless, helpless, without God and eternally damned unless he embraces Christianity by faith in the finished work of Christ. To the sinner, nothing is pure.

To hear the Gospel and reject it is enough sin to damn any poor sinner. It is not eating, drinking, nor participating in ungodly lust that damns the sinner; but "He that believeth not is condemned already, because he hath not believed in the name of the only begotten Son of God."

To the unbeliever, everything is made the means of increasing his depravity, his unrighteousness and his ungodliness. It makes no difference what ordinances of religion unbelievers may observe or practice. It matters not what distinctions they may make concerning meats, drinks, days, ceremonies, or religious events. Such observances will not change their state of depravity. Making distinctions in foods, drinks, and clothing only fosters pride and produces self-righteousness. Those who do these things are attempting to justify themselves through their own goodness and labors, following the commandments of men instead of submitting to the love of God. They push aside the mercies of God and satisfy their own lusts. They are corrupt at heart, and observance of ordinances, ceremonies, abstinence from food and drink makes them no better. It simply leads to deeper depravity and greater condemnation.

This defilement goes much deeper than outward defilement of the body. The mind and conscience, the very inner man, is defiled, polluted, and rotten. Every action leads to greater corruption, and the inner man becomes more and more despicable in the sight of a righteous God. An unbeliever does not remain the same. Day by day he becomes worse, and regardless how much good he may seem to be doing, the Scripture tells us that "we are all as an unclean thing, and all our righteousnesses are as filthy rags" (Isaiah 64:6).

Verse fifteen, then, in effect repeats the Lord's teaching that it is what comes out of a man that defiles him, not ceremonial impurity. The real seat of purity is the conscience, and if defilement has entered there, mind and action are alike affected.

Those who make a false profession of religion often strongly avow their knowledge of God, and this was particularly true of those with Judaistic tendencies. These Jewish professors in religion claimed that they had a

Dealing with Gainsayers   255

singular knowledge concerning God. Nine times a day they would shout the Shema: "Hear O Israel, the Lord our God is one Lord." There was a great Judaistic pride in monotheism.

While these Jewish false prophets claimed God with their lips, they denied God with their works. They thought they had a special unique relationship with God, when in fact they denied Him. Words of strong condemnation are richly deserved and the apostle uses three such words to characterize their conduct. It is interesting that all three terms relate to the law in which they boasted.

First, they were abominable. The meaning of the word is "detestable, to be held in abhorrence." In our language, "a debased, despicable, deplorable, disgusting person." Throughout the Old Testament, God would call impure things abominations. It is ironic that those who claimed to track down disgusting things are themselves disgusting.

Second, they are disobedient. They have violated the commandments of a holy God who demanded holiness in the law.

Then third, they are reprobate. The word signifies "not standing the test, rejected of God." All their good works in which they boasted are found to be deficient. All who make a profession and submit themselves for ordination must be tested. These gainsayers, upon testing, are found to be deficient for any good work. I have seen some of God's dear pastors bring heartache and tragedy upon themselves by using little precaution in selecting leaders in the church. A church would be better off with no deacons at all, or with only two or three, than with men appointed to the board when they do not qualify for that office. Better had the pastor teach the entire Sunday School than to appoint teachers who sow seeds of error and live lives that are not spiritual. Yes, there are those today who stand in the way of sinners and sit in the seat of the scornful and they must be dealt with accordingly.

CHAPTER TWENTY-NINE

Dealing with Old People

Titus 2:1-3

In chapter one, Paul instructed Titus concerning the organization of local churches in the various cities of the island of Crete and warned him to be extremely cautious in selecting bishops in the local assembly. In chapter two, however, Paul gives Titus instructions regarding his own responsibility to the believers in the local assemblies and the method he is to employ in teaching the pure Gospel.

The Basis of the Pastor's Teaching (v. 1)

This verse stands in stark contrast to the last verse of chapter one. Whereas the false teachers were making empty professions, Titus is to speak the things which become sound doctrine. The word translated "become" is the Greek word *prepei* which means "to be suitable, fitting." Titus is to teach the things which are in compliance with sound doctrine.

We notice that Paul has already mentioned sound doctrine in 1:9. Then he describes the gainsayers in 1:10-16. Now he mentions sound doctrine again in 2:1. On either side of his remarks concerning false teachers, Paul has mentioned sound doctrine. The best way that Titus can combat the disease of heresy that was troubling the church was by combatting it with sound or healthy doctrine.

The distinction between that which is right and that which is wrong in theology should always be distinctly made. The "thou" in verse one is emphatic in order to emphasize that Titus belongs to a very different category from the troublemakers. That distinction is to be maintained.

It can only be maintained if Titus speaks the things which are in compliance with sound doctrine. In other words, "Titus, do not incorporate your own ideas or opinions into your message when you preach. Teach the things that are doctrinally sound. Do not add anything to the Gospel you have heard, and do not take away from it."

In this day and hour, many times an esteemed clergyman steps behind the sacred desk on Sunday morning and reads a little essay. He opens by saying, "In my humble opinion." God is not concerned, however, about your opinion or mine. He is not concerned about the way we see things. Regardless of what a particular minister may think or say about it, opinions are not worth anything. God said it, it stands, and we must believe it.

Titus was to preach nothing that was opposed to the Word of God nor anything that deviates from it. He is to preach "Thus saith the Lord." He is not to incorporate tradition, fables, dogma, or the commandments of men into his message. He is to preach the Bible, minus man's ideas and superstitions. The Word of God was to be the basis of his message.

The Beneficiaries of the Pastor's Teaching (vv. 2-3)

The Old Gentlemen (v. 2)

The first practical outworking of such sound doctrine will be an insistence that behavior should tally with belief. If people really believe sound doctrine, they will function in certain ways. So, Paul tells Titus to teach certain ages and sexes certain things, not because Christian morality differs depending how old you are or what sex you are, but because different ages and sexes are more prone to certain errors.

The first place where Paul tells Titus to begin is with the older men. Their actions are to become senior members of the community. The first three qualities which he lists here are qualities which are generally expected from men in advancing age.

First, they are to be sober. The Greek word *nephalios* is used not merely of restraint in the use of wine, but moderation in general.

Then they are to be grave, a seriousness of purpose particularly suits the dignity of seniors. The word *grave* combines the ideas of gravity and dignity. It denotes that which inspires reverence and awe. Aged men are not to enter their second childhood and act like a child again from the standpoint of frivolous thinking and foolish practices. They must act their age in all things. This does not mean, however, that they have to act gloomy all time.

Then third, the aged men are to be temperate. The Greek word *sophron* points to self-control. They must be masters of themselves. Just because they are nearing the end of life's journey does not give them a license to be intemperate in anything: eating, drinking, or any other phase of daily living.

Not only do we see in this passage a triad of self-restraining qualities. We also see a triad of Christian virtues. First, they are to be sound in faith. They must be careful that the enemy does not plant seeds of unfaithfulness, causing them to go off on a tangent. I have seen so many older men go off on a theological tangent in their older years. It is easy for the devil to play tricks on the mind if we do not keep our minds entirely centered in the Word of God and in the faith once delivered to the saints.

The aged believer must also be sound in charity. By this time in life he should have overcome all the fiery, impetuous, envious, wrathful, passions of his earlier years. The longer we live for Jesus, the sweeter we should become in the Lord. There are times when the aged men become unhappy. They grumble, and they become unlovely. Do not allow the devil to mar your beautiful Christian testimony by becoming a grouch or a grumbler. "Rejoice in the Lord, alway, and again I say rejoice."

Then finally the aged men should be patient. For Paul, the cardinal Christian virtues are faith, hope, and love but patience is not so far removed from hope as to cause a difficulty. Paul substitutes patience for hope

Dealing with Old People

here because he is thinking especially of old men, whose attitude to life is now one of resignation. Aged believers should submit to the trials, the heartaches, and the disappointments of their advanced years, knowing that Jesus said, "I will never leave thee nor forsake thee." Look to Jesus, not at circumstances around you. Keep in mind that this may be the day when the trumpet will sound. If the Lord should delay His coming, it will not be long until you renew your youth before the throne of God. Be sound in patience.

It is interesting to note that the Greek word *hugiaino* which means "to be sound" is used of elderly men's pursuit of Christian graces, and it is also used of doctrine in verse one. Both heart and mind for the Christian must function in a healthy manner.

The Elderly Ladies (v. 3)

In introducing the subject of elderly women the apostle uses the adverb hosautos. This word which is translated "likewise" is a favorite expression of Paul's in the pastorals. It brings out the closeness of comparison with what precedes. As the older men were to meet their requirements, so the older women are to meet these requirements.

First, they are to have behavior which becomes holiness. This is a phrase which contains two Greek words unique in the New Testament. The first word *katastema* means "demeanour." It describes a state of mind. The second word *hieroprepes* means "suited to a sacred character." In other words, older ladies are to be reverent in their demeanor.

Second, they are not to be false accusers. In I Timothy 3:11 the same word is used and is there translated "slanderers." The aged women are to be careful how they use their tongues in the community. They are not to be false in their conversation concerning fellow church members, nor even concerning unbelievers. They are to tell the truth at all times, and be silent if they cannot speak those things which become holiness. They should not be gossipers.

Third, they should not be given to much wine. The verb here *doulo* signifies bondage. They should not be slaves to drink. The Greek suggests that it means that these women are not to talk and act like women who linger over wine. Wine causes one to talk who ordinarily may be silent, and wine will cause one to make statements that are false or exaggerated. Therefore, the aged, believing women are not to act like women who sit long at wine.

Then finally, they are to be teachers of good things. Obviously, the context here does not apply to public speaking. It rather refers to ministry in the home. Within this sphere, experienced Christian women have throughout the history of the church performed invaluable service in the cause of Christ by their example and teaching. They are to instruct the younger women in the faith. Seasoned believers among the female sex should be instructed to teach younger women and girls in the graces of Christian femininity.

CHAPTER THIRTY

Dealing with Young Ladies

Titus 2:4-5

Titus' ministry to young women is not to be a direct ministry. He is to teach old men directly (v. 2), old ladies directly (v. 3), and young men directly (v. 6). He is not, however, to teach young ladies directly. They are to be taught by the older women. Thus, the pastor's ministry to older ladies is twofold. First, he is to teach them how to behave, and then he is to teach them how to teach the younger women.

The Young Ladies Responsibilities to Themselves (vv. 4a, 5a, 5c)

In his list of characteristics which are to be found in young ladies, several apply to the lady's responsibility to herself. The first of these is that the young lady is to be sober. The Greek word translated "sober" is the same word translated "temperate" in verse two, and it is the same word used in I Timothy 3:2 of pastors. The meaning of the Greek word is that the aged women should instruct the younger women to have their desires and passions well under control and regulated.

Many times when a young lady gets married, she automatically assumes that her new husband will be able to lavish her with the luxuries provided by her father. She gets married with unrealistic expectations. Paul tells the older women to teach the younger women to

263

put those desires and passions under control. Regulate them. Be sober.

The second responsibility of the young lady with regards to herself is that of being discreet. It is interesting that the Greek word underlying "discreet" is the same word translated "temperate" in verse two and "sober" in verse four. This is the second time this word is used in reference to young ladies. The first time the word is used of young ladies, it is used in a context of love. In other words, ladies are to be controlled as to whom they love. They must be careful not to love other men, but rather to thrust their love upon their husbands and their children.

The second time the word is used, however, it is used in the context of being domesticated. They are to be controlled as far as not pursuing a career or glamour, but rather they are to invest their energies in being keepers at home and maintaining obedience to their husbands.

Then these young ladies are to be chaste. Every time this word is used in the New Testament, it is used as a synonym for purity. Young women are to be pure in heart and in every detail of life. They are to be the picture of purity.

Then the final quality with regards to themselves is goodness. In all respects and in all relations, the wife and mother must be good. There can be no greater compliment paid to a woman, no higher characteristic ascribed to her, than to say, "She is good." The greatest compliment God ever gives is a commendation of goodness.

Many times when this word is used in the New Testament, it is used in the sense of being kind (cf. Matthew 20:15). The sweetest creation on the face of the earth is a sweet woman. The most precious thing this side of heaven is a godly wife or mother, but the meanest creature this side of hell is a mean woman. Young women should try their best to be kind.

The Young Ladies Responsibilities to Their Families (vv. 4b, 5b, 5d)

The first responsibility the young lady has to her family is to love her husband. In Ephesians 5:25, the Apostle Paul commands husbands to love their own wives. Here in our present verse, Paul simply points out that the young woman should love her husband which is her first duty to him. All true happiness in marriage is based on mutual love. The husband loves the wife with all of his heart, and the wife loves the husband in like manner.

It matters not how wealthy the couple may be. They may live in a mansion, but wealth and a magnificent home cannot bring happiness where there is no love, or where love has cooled on the part of either husband or wife. Regardless of how humble the home may be, whether in the city or remote countryside, if mutual love exists between husband and wife, that home is a suburb of heaven. The house may be a mansion, the furniture the finest, and the couple may fare sumptuously every day, but if two hearts are not knit together in love, that mansion is a hell on earth.

Women are also to love their children. Now this is very important. Most animals will fight and die to protect their young, but some men and women are so totally depraved that they lose all respect and love for their own flesh and blood, their children. The aged saints are to teach the younger women to love their children. Any precious mother with a baby in the home has a full time job twenty-four hours a day, seven days a week. No other person will ever love your child as you love it if you are a true mother. No other person can train or discipline that child as you will if you are a true mother. No person can take the place of a mother. Therefore, mothers should love their children above fame, fortune, beauty, houses, or social prestige. Children should come above all these things. A mother should forsake all except her husband to give love, time, and attention to her children. The best friend any child will ever have on the face of this earth is a godly, consecrated mother who loves him.

It is natural for a mother to love her children, but some mothers love the night club, the wine bottle, and the arms of another man more than they love their own flesh and blood. There are thousands of poodles and cats that receive the attention and caresses that a baby should be receiving.

I am not against pets, but they should be kept in their place and should never take the place of a child in the home. There are thousands of homes where children are not wanted and thousands of married women who refuse to permit children to come into the home

Dealing with Young Ladies 267

because a baby would interfere with their career and with social activities. These women often substitute pets for a child.

Some Christian wives refuse to permit a family. They are dedicated to their job, their social activities, their career, and sometimes (believe it or not) their pets. Strange, but true, some wives do need to be taught to love their children.

In view of the disturbance the false teachers were bringing to families (1:11), this injunction was very important. Even in our modern age we see numerous Christian women lacking true maternal affection. Women who put their careers before the welfare of their own children display this weakness. When I asked Karen to be my wife, I asked her at the very same time to be the mother of my children. Young women are to love their children.

Now in keeping with this, young women are to be keepers at home. A young married woman's sphere is the home. She is not to neglect the duties of the home in order to participate in things outside the home. In other words, she is not to be better known outside the home than in the home, by her own husband and family. The word *keeper* here implies "diligence." She is to be diligent at home, not lazy or slothful, not unconcerned about the home and the things pertaining thereto. She is to give her best to the home, seeing that things are in order and that the home is kept as becomes a Christian.

I don't like to say that Christian women should not work because that gives the impression that housewives sit around all day doing nothing. A Christian woman is to be a worker, but the sphere where she is to work is the home. This is the place where the Bible says she is to be diligent. She is not to be diligent investing most of her energies for a corporation somewhere. Her energies are to be invested in the home. That is the place where she is to be diligent.

A woman who is a believer should take pride in her home. She should keep that home clean, neat, and presentable. A young married woman with a baby and a home, if she does her duty, has a full-time job.

Never forget that God made the woman to make this world a sweeter, brighter, happier place in which to live. Adam was lonely; his life was empty. He found not a helper as he named the animals. Therefore, God removed a rib from Adam's side and made Eve, and gave her to Adam to be a help suitable for him. A young woman who is not willing to make a home for her husband and her family should stay single.

Regardless of how much a mother may do outside the home, whatever self-denial and zeal she may contribute to outside interests, and regardless of how much good she may accomplish outside the home, if she neglects her home she has brought reproach upon Christianity. The duty of a Christian mother is first to her home, and these other interests must be secondary.

The last family requirement for a young lady is for her to be obedient to her own husband (cf. Ephesians 5:22). God created Adam and gave him dominion over everything. Man is the head of the woman, and the wife is to be obedient to her own husband in all things (Colossians 3:18). God created woman for a specific purpose, but He did not create her to rule man. Any home, any church, or any nation that is ruled by a woman is headed for destruction.

The Reason for the Young Ladies Responsibilities (v. 5e)

Young women are to be careful to maintain these characteristics, especially in home life, for a specific purpose. This purpose is that the Word of God be not blasphemed. Contravention of these Christian qualities would be a denial of the Word of God which these women professed to believe.

It would be an affront to the Christian message. When women are emancipated by the Gospel, they should not abuse that new-found liberty in ways violating the Word of God, even if these ways are approved by contemporary society.

As grand and glorious as is the privilege of being a wife and mother, so grave, great, and weighty is the responsibility. Woe be to the woman who professes to be a godly mother, but in her home activity denies that she is in her heart what she professes with her lips. Never entertain the idea that we can profess one thing and live another.

Christian matrons are to assist the younger women in the discipline of family love, not of course as interfering busybodies, but as humble advisors on problems of married life. This instruction has a very important purpose: that the Word of God be not blasphemed.

CHAPTER THIRTY-ONE

Dealing with Young Men

Titus 2:6-8

The Exhortation (v. 6)

Attention is now focused on the young men, in whose case the special exhortation is once again directed toward self-mastery. Titus is to exhort them to be sober-minded. The word here translated "exhort" is the Greek word *parakaleo*. It is the same word used of the Holy Spirit in John's gospel. The word is a much stronger term than the word translated "speak" in verse one. Elderly men are to be spoken to, but younger men are to be urged to control themselves. The construction here emphasizes the need for constant moral reminders.

These young men should by all means surrender soul, spirit, and body unreservedly unto God, and they should master their appetites and passions, thereby being good examples of the believer, not bringing reproach upon the church and upon the Saviour. Since they are Christians, they should set up self-government in their own hearts and lives. They should set standards for themselves that would bring glory to God, and then trust God for strength, grace, and power to live up to those standards.

It has sometimes been supposed that there is nothing distinctively Christian about such advice as it is given here. Self-control was an element of Greek ethics,

271

and many liberals believe that Paul is simply borrowing from Greek ethics here. The self-mastery of the Christian, however, has an element of humility lacking in the Greek moralists. True Christian self-control is actually Spirit-control because the fruit of the Spirit is temperance (Galatians 5:22-23).

The Holy Spirit will give to the young man strength and courage to have a well-governed mind, which in the hour of temptation will keep him from indulging in passions to which the young are tempted and prone to succumb. Young men who name the name of Jesus should be steady in their behavior, solid in their belief, superior to sensual temptations, constant in the exercise of self-government. If young men succumb to the lusts of the flesh and the temptations thereof, sooner or later these lusts will destroy the body, which is the tabernacle of God (cf. I Thessalonians 5:23).

The Example (v. 7)

Titus, as a Christian minister, must be a pattern of good works. The word translated "pattern" was initially used of the impress of a die. Hence the word was used in a metaphorical sense of an example. The exhortations of Titus would carry no weight unless they were backed up by the pattern of his life, a principle which has been amply illustrated in the history of Christian ministry. It is a high demand to show an example in all things, but no less than this suffices for the Christian minister.

The word *doctrine* should probably be understood in its active sense. The reference here then refers to the

Dealing with Young Men

act of teaching, the delivery of the sermon. Verse eight is going to deal with the content of the sermon; verse seven deals with its delivery. Titus is not merely to teach others with words, but his pulpit demeanor is also a powerful teaching tool. Titus should show the young men, by example, how to live.

There are three things which are mentioned concerning Titus' sermon delivery. The first is that the sermon is to be incorrupt. The underlying word is unique in Biblical Greek, and it denotes "untaintedness." Titus is not to allow any erroneous doctrine to be preached or taught in the assemblies in Crete. Only pure doctrine, free from all error, can be allowed. Titus was to preach the Gospel that would make men pure, better men, and sound doctrine does just that. So in his delivery, Titus was not to be guilty of any Titusisms. He was to make sure that all his sermons were carefully based on the Bible.

Second, the sermon is to be delivered with gravity. Titus' sermons are to possess a note of seriousness. The Christian teacher must teach in a serious manner if his words are to earn respect. The meaning here is that the manner in which God's preacher delivers the message God has given him should be a manner to command the respect of the listeners. His message should evidence good sense, undoubted piety, and should demonstrate that he is acquainted with the subject, proving that he has spent much time in study and prayer. The message should be serious, simple, and delivered with all earnestness. It is a great and grave responsibility for God's preacher to stand in the pulpit and deliver God's Word to men and women who are eternity-bound.

Then finally, Titus' sermons are to be delivered with sincerity. The underlying Greek word is translated "immortality" in Romans 2:7 and II Timothy 1:10. In I Corinthians 15:42, 50, 53, and 54, it is translated "incorruption." The word literally means "deathlessness." In early times, the word had the wide connotation of freedom from death. In the New Testament, the word expresses more than deathlessness. It suggests the quality of life enjoyed. In II Corinthians 5:4, the concept of immortality is a cause for rejoicing. The idea then is that the preacher's sermons should be full of life and joy.

So, there is a delicate balance here. The pastor's sermons are not to be frivolous, comprised only of jokes and humor, but that does not mean that the sermon should come across as a dead fish either. The sermons should be joyful and full of life.

The Eloquence (v. 8)

Whereas the spotlight so far has been turned mainly on Titus' actions, it is now transferred to his teaching. The order is significant. Example comes before precept, but the precept which follows example must be of the noblest kind. In verse seven, the manner of his teaching was to be untainted, and now in verse eight, the matter of his teaching is to be sound or wholesome.

The word *sound* is commonly applied to the body meaning that which is healthy or whole. Titus was to teach, preach, and use language that would be help-

Dealing with Young Men 275

ful and healthy from a spiritual standpoint. Paul wanted Titus to speak only sound words that would edify, strengthen, and build up believers, and keep them healthy and clean spiritually.

If Titus was doing this, he would be speaking words which could not be condemned. He would be preaching a gospel with which no one could find fault. This teaching would be irreprehensible. Titus must ensure that he gives no occasion for these gainsayers to level an accusation against himself or his teaching. By exemplary life and speech, Titus can make those opposed to him ashamed. This would only happen if Titus presented sermons which demonstrated solidity in spiritual argument.

The last part of this verse simply states a fact which will be true if Titus preaches the Gospel as laid down by the Apostle Paul. The enemy will be ashamed that he opposed such a message, because the Word of God will not return void; it will accomplish that whereunto it is sent. Any minister who defends the faith and preaches the pure Gospel of the marvelous grace of God will never be forced to apologize for the message he has delivered, because it will always bring forth fruit. Paul wanted Titus to be a fruitful minister; he wanted those to whom Titus preached to be healthy, strong believers.

So, the concluding words "having no evil thing to say of you" are not suggesting that the opponents will find no words with which to abuse the Christian minister, but they are suggesting that the Christian minister should present no opportunity for his opponents legitimately to use an evil report against him.

Titus is to exhort the young men to be self-controlled. This admonition, however, will only be followed if Titus proves himself a worthy mentor. Since the vast majority of opinion is formulated about a minister based on his pulpit ministry, that is where Titus should especially be careful. Both in how he teaches and in what he teaches he is to be an example to the young men.

CHAPTER THIRTY-TWO

Dealing with Servants

Titus 2:9-10

As in writing to Timothy, so now in advising Titus, the apostle finds it necessary to deal with the problem of slavery. He lays down some principles governing their relationship with masters, but the injunctions are slightly varied.

The Principle of Submission (v. 9a)

It is significant that, whereas in Ephesians and Colossians Paul urges servants to obey their masters, here alone he uses the verb *hupotasso* which means "to be in subjection." This latter word is the strongest, perhaps suggesting a greater tendency on the part of Christian slaves in Crete to abuse their new-found emancipation in Christ. Presumably, the injunction applies primarily to slaves with Christian masters, but it should not be limited to that. Servants were to submit to their masters, even if those masters were abusive (cf. I Peter 3:18).

In Paul's day, there were still many slaves and slave-masters. Some of the masters had been saved, while others had not. Hundreds of slaves had been born again, and Paul knew that if the Christian slaves did not render the right kind of obedience and service to their masters, they would be poor testimonies for the grace of God. Therefore, he wanted the servants who were believers to be obedient to their masters, to serve them well, to

277

please them in all things, and not to be disputing or arguing with them because such a servant would never influence his master to become a believer. Paul knew that the believing servants could win their masters if they would prove to them that Christianity saves, satisfies, and brings peace that passes all understanding, peace that position and money cannot attain.

The phrase "to please them well in all things" does not mean that the servant is to dishonor God in order to please his master, but only insofar as pleasing his earthly master does not contradict his belief in the heavenly master. The Christian servant was not to do anything morally or spiritually wrong to please his master, but neither was he to do anything to antagonize his master, because of his faith in God. He was to do all in his power to win his master by daily demonstrating the peace of God in his heart, the testimony of God from his lips, and in service rendered to his master. He was not to be a disobedient servant, contradicting his master, nor rendering half-hearted, slovenly service. He was to do what his master required so long as it did not interfere with a godly conscience.

Slaves were to please their masters well in everything. They were to give them satisfaction all around. The word here translated "please well" is the Greek word *euarestos*, and is mostly used in the New Testament of being well-pleasing to God. If Christian slaves could introduce into their lives so high a principle as this, it would do much to lessen the evils of the system and to show the power of Christianity to transform the most difficult relationships.

Dealing with Servants

The Practice of Submission (vv. 9b-10a)

There are several ways a slave could implement this principle of submission. The first way is by not answering again. The prohibition against answering again should probably be understood in the wider sense of opposition. Slaves should not do anything that would thwart their masters' plans.

He was not to put forth his own opinion and argue any matter with the master, recognizing the fact that he was a servant and that he was to obey, not to reason and instruct. To sum it up, the servant was to obey his master in everything that is not contrary to the will of God. He is to do this without contradicting or disputing the matter.

There was another way that slaves could practice submission that was by abstaining from purloining. The word here translated "purloining" is the Greek word *nosphizo* which was the regular term in Greek for petty larcenies, a vice to which slaves would be particularly tempted. The word *purloin* then means to take or carry away another's property for one's own use, and would be applied to anything belonging to the employer, which a servant might take for himself. The servant was not to appropriate to his own use anything that belonged to his master. Of course, this sin has been prevalent among servants down through the years. Many times a servant feels that he does not receive what is due him, and therefore he takes it. Paul is here instructing Titus to preach against this vice which is, in plain words, nothing less than stealing, and it is a sin to steal.

The positive side of this is that the slave is to show all good fidelity. This is the positive side of honesty. Masters should be able to put good faith in their servants. The verb here "show forth" carries with it the idea of providing proof. Servants should prove themselves worthy of their master's good faith.

In laboring and in taking care of the property or whatever the master instructs the servant or slave to do, a believing servant should care for and protect his master's property as carefully as though it were his own. He should prove himself worthy of good faith.

The Purpose of Submission (v. 10b)

The concluding statement in verse 10 gives the dominating principle which raises these injunctions to slaves to a much higher level than contemporary Greek ethics. Slaves must act in this way for a definite purpose, and that purpose is to adorn the doctrine of God. The verb *cosmeo* from which we get our word *cosmetic* was used of the arrangement of jewels in a manner to set off their full beauty. This idea is emphasized here. By exemplary Christian conduct, a slave has the power to enhance the doctrine of Christianity and to make it appear beautiful in the eyes of onlookers. Such a principle as this is by no means confined to slaves.

It is applicable to all Christians in all walks of life. The words "in all things" could possibly be masculine with the sense of "among all men." This would illustrate the opportunity for slaves to permeate every part of society with their witness.

Dealing with Servants

The servant must show the fair influence of Christianity on him in all respects. He should show that Christianity makes him more industrious, more honest, and more obedient. Christian servants were not to be hateful and argumentative, but kind and considerate, showing that they were better fitted to perform their duties, regardless of how humble those duties might be.

These believing servants were to show that the Christian religion definitely changed every detail of their life and that they are better servants because of their Christian belief. By their labors and attitude toward their masters, they were to prove what they believed in their hearts. By this conduct they might hope to win their masters to Christianity and cause them to see that the Gospel does make a change in the life of the one who believes.

Regardless of how insignificant one may feel, one in the humblest walk of life may so live as to be an ornament to Christianity, a sign board that advertises well the profit of being a Christian. Those in humble positions may be used of God just as greatly as those who may be favored with many more advantages.

Paul is teaching here that servants may do tremendous good by living daily in such a way that their lives will be epistles read by men. They should be living sermons in their actions and attitudes toward their slave master, or toward the person to whom they are in service.

CHAPTER THIRTY-THREE

The Grace of God

Titus 2:11-15

Throughout chapter two, Paul has been giving Titus various regulations for members in the church. There have been regulations for aged men, aged women, young women, young men, and slaves. Now Paul is going to conclude this chapter by giving Titus a theological reason for demanding such conduct. There is a close connection in the New Testament between theology and ethics. The word translated "for" in verse eleven is an explanatory *gar*. Paul is going to explain the statement that we should adorn the doctrine of God our Saviour. Notice that Paul in talking about adorning Christian doctrine speaks of God as Saviour. Christ not only saves us from the penalty of sin, He saves us from the power of sin. This mentioning of God as Saviour leads Paul naturally to discuss briefly the nature of our salvation, which if understood, will produce godly conduct.

The grace of God redeems (vv. 11, 14)

Paul in verse eleven gives a concise statement concerning both the incarnation and the atonement. Paul begins by personifying grace and tells us that this grace of God has appeared. The word translated "appeared" is the Greek word *epiphaino*. Paul often uses the cognate noun *epiphaneia* to refer to the Second Advent. Here, however, the context clearly refers to the first advent,

283

and the grace of God is personified in the person of the Lord Jesus Christ.

The expression "the grace of God" may be said to be the key phrase of Paul's theology. He cannot think of Christian salvation apart from the grace of God. We can define grace in this context as God's free favor in Christ in dealing with man's sin. In verse eleven, we learn that the grace of God brings salvation, and that apart from grace there is no salvation. We are saved by God's grace (Ephesians 2:8-9). Grace brings salvation. Salvation does not become ours through sincere living, giving, praying, begging, or abstaining. The grace of God brings salvation to the heart of the believer.

Clearly the dative here "to all men" does not reference the incarnation. When Jesus appeared on this earth, he did not appear to all men. The phrase "to all men", therefore, in the most natural interpretation of the Greek construction refers to the term *salvation*. The grace of God has appeared bringing salvation to all men. Thus, we learn that there is no such thing as limited atonement. There are many outstanding religionists who teach and preach that some are elected to be saved, while others are not elected to be saved. According to these teachers, if you are not elected, you cannot be saved; there is no need to try. They teach and preach that if you are elected, you will be saved, and if you are not elected, you cannot be saved. Our present verse tells us that that the grace of God which brings salvation has appeared to all men. Jesus came to save "whosoever will."

The Grace of God 285

This atonement is described for us in a multi-faceted way in verse fourteen. The first thing we notice about the atonement is that it was a voluntary sacrifice. We see here the sacrificial character of Christ's act. He gave Himself. He was not forced or driven; He willingly laid down His life (John 10:17-18).

This voluntary sacrifice was also a substitutionary death. Christ gave Himself for us. Certainly, the preposition *huper* brings out the sacrificial character and the substitionary nature of Christ's death. It was in our place on our behalf that He died.

Also, in this one verse Christ's death is defined as a redemption. The verb used here is *lutroo* which means "to release on receipt of a ransom." There is redemption in no other than the Lord Jesus Christ. The blood of Jesus Christ, God's Son, cleanses us from all sin. It is in Jesus that we have redemption. Without the shedding of His blood there is no remission of sin (I Peter 1:18-20). He gave Himself that He might redeem us.

The special aspect of verse fourteen, however, where Paul wants to spend the majority of his time is on the purpose of that redemption. The purpose of that redemption was to redeem us from all iniquity. A holy God demands holiness. Nothing shall enter that city that defiles. Only the pure and spotless shall be there. Such purity could be provided only by a holy God. Therefore, God gave Jesus (and Jesus gave Himself) to redeem us from all iniquity and make us pure. The redemption that is ours in Christ Jesus did not simply redeem us out of sin, but it redeemed us from sinning.

The point is that we are saved not only from the penalty of sin, but also from its power.

There is a sanctifying and cleansing element in the atonement. This act of purification is performed by Christ Himself (Ephesians 5:25-26). Here we clearly see that Christ's self-giving sacrifice is intricately linked with His sanctifying work.

Christ has purified us unto Himself. We have been saved for Christ's sake (Ephesians 4:32). Jesus redeemed us unto Himself, and we who make up the true church are His peculiar treasure. Believers are a peculiar people, not strange, but peculiar. The word means "one's own possession." It means that we are to be regarded as belonging to the Lord Jesus Christ.

This has all been said for one reason. The reason that we have been chosen, the reason we have been made God's peculiar people, is so we can show forth the praises of Him who has called us out of darkness (cf. I Peter 2:9). Believers are peculiar in that they do not love the things of the world or practice them. They do not see or feel as does the world. They are peculiar in the respect that they are unlike others. They are zealous of good works.

Paul uses this underlying Greek word *zelotes* in Galatians 1:14 of his own eagerness to maintain the traditions of his ancestors. Although this zeal was misplaced, Paul never lost his enthusiasm, and he envisages here a whole people noted for rightly directed zeal. This is what God's grace has chosen us for (Ephesians 2:8-10).

True faith produces works. We are not saved by

works, but we work when we are saved. God does not expect all believers to be full-time ministers, but all believers are to be full-time Christians. We are to work if we are saved. Certainly, this puts some religionists and church members in difficult circumstances, because many of them claim to have been saved for many years, yet they never work for the Lord. They have never proved their salvation by their works. Works do not save us, but works prove that we are saved; and the grace of God teaches us to be zealous of good works

The grace of God reforms (vv. 12, 15)

In our present verse, we learn that the grace of God not only brings salvation, but the grace of God that saves us immediately sets up a classroom in our hearts and becomes the teacher. Grace is here personified in its task of educating us in the art of living, and, as so often in the pastoral epistles, attention is drawn to both negative and positive aspects of a Christian's education. There must be a double denial, first of ungodliness, and then of worldly lusts. Then there must be the positive elements of soberness, righteousness, and godliness.

The grace of God teaches us first to deny ungodliness. Just what is ungodliness? Anything that is not godly is ungodly. Anything that does not bring praise, adoration, and honor to God certainly brings disgrace and dishonor upon His name. Therefore, anything that is not godly and to God's glory can be classified under ungodliness.

Grace, the divine teacher which brings salvation

to our hearts, goes further. It also teaches us to deny worldly lusts. What is worldly lusts? It is anything the eyes gaze upon which would draw us away from God. When the flesh craves that which is unholy and unrighteous, that is worldly lusts. All desires centered in this present world's system must be denied.

Ungodliness here means all that would be included under the word *impiety*. That is, all failure on the part of the believer in the performance of proper duties and practices by the believer toward God. Worldly lusts here refers to any and all things that are improper having to do with desires, habits, and appetites of this life.

God's grace teaches us to deny these things. Notice that the negative (in a Christian's life) precedes the positive here. We deny these things in order to live the kind of life we should by living and practicing the things described in the last part of verse twelve. We are not saved by denying ungodliness and worldly lusts. The positive precedes the negative as having to do with redemption; but for the man who is already saved, the negative precedes the positive.

The first positive is that we are to live soberly. This means that we should exercise due restraint on our passions and practices of daily living. We should be sober, not only in abstinence from alcohol, but in our appetites, passions, and anything that would draw us away from godliness and right living.

Then we are to live righteously or justly referring to the proper performance of our duties as having to do with our fellow man. It means that in our daily living,

The Grace of God   289

Christianity teaches us to perform all duties in relation to our fellow citizens and neighbors.

Then the grace of God teaches us to live godly. That is, piously, not self-righteously. We are to live piously in the faithful performance of our duties to God. This third requirement is the exact counterpart of the first denial. It is not enough to renounce ungodliness; life must be lived in a godly manner. So, the Christian should live a virtuous life with regards to himself (soberly), with regards to his neighbor (righteously), and with regards to God (godly).

This is to be done in this present world. We should be what we ought to be for Jesus right now. We are saved now. In this present world, we are now the sons of God (I John 3:1-3). It is altogether possible for a believer to deny ungodliness and worldly lusts. It is possible for the believer, and normal for the believer, to live soberly, righteously, and godly right here in this present world.

This is what Titus was to preach. Titus is to declare these things, by which is meant presumably all the injunctions in chapter two. In addition to speaking, the Christian minister is to engage in exhortation and reproof (cf. II Timothy 4:2). Some will require encouragement, and others censure, but whatever the need Titus is to exercise all authority. This word is found elsewhere in the New Testament only in the Pauline epistles and always in the sense of a divine command. Here Paul means that the Christian minister is endowed with nothing less than divine authority. Titus need not fear, therefore, to exercise jurisdiction over those entrusted to him. Some would no doubt attempt to despise him, but he is to demonstrate the seal of God upon his ministry. Titus was to preach these things without compromise without keeping anything back. He was to preach them, not simply as advice or counsel from a minister, but as the command of God. He was to preach these things without fear or favor, and to do it with all authority.

God's minister does not need to apologize for preaching grace, pure grace, and only grace for salvation. God's minister need not apologize for preaching against ungodliness and worldly lusts, naming these sins to those whom he preaches. God's minister steps in the pulpit to preach sober, righteous, godly living right here in this present world. He does it with authority and without apology. These things speak, exhort, and rebuke with all authority. Do not apologize.

Now whenever a preacher starts preaching on sin, calling it what it is, people will inevitably state, "I wish that preacher would preach on grace." Well, the grace of God not only brings salvation; it also teaches us to deny ungodliness and worldly lusts and live soberly, righteously, and godly in this present world. So if you want grace, here it is. The grace of God reforms.

The grace of God rewards (v. 13)

Verse twelve closed with a reference to this present world, but the Christian also looks to the future. The grace of God also teaches us to look for that blessed hope. I do not hesitate to make the next statement. All believers believe in the second coming of Jesus Christ.

The Grace of God 291

We may not all agree on every detail of prophecy concerning His second coming, but if we are born again, we are recipients of God's grace. If we are recipients of God's grace, then grace teaches us to look for that blessed hope.

In Hebrews 9:28 we read that Jesus is coming for those who look for Him, and the grace of God teaches us to look for that blessed hope. If you do not believe in the second coming of Christ and if you are not looking for His return, it all adds up to the clear fact that you are not saved. God's grace that brings salvation teaches us to look for Jesus.

The second coming of Jesus is, to the believer, that blessed hope. In the New Testament, hope does not indicate merely what is wished for but what is assured. We have a blessed assurance. The second coming was never intended to be a frightening doctrine for believers. In I Thessalonians 4:13-18, Paul closes this great portion of Scripture on the Rapture with this admonition: "Wherefore comfort one another with these words." The second coming of Jesus Christ is a comforting hope, an assuring hope. It is blessed and most precious to the believer.

It will be a glorious day for the believer. It will be when the bodies of believers who have died will be raised incorruptible. Those of us who are living when Jesus comes in the Rapture will be changed in a moment, in the twinkling of an eye. These mortal bodies will put on immortality, and we will have a body just like the body of Jesus.

That will be a glorious event for believers, because we will see Jesus face to face. We will sit down at the marriage supper in the sky. We will be rewarded for our stewardship, and we will return to this earth to reign with Him for one thousand years.

The hope of the church is the glorious appearing of the great God and our Saviour, Jesus Christ. The church is in the world, but not of it. Our citizenship is heaven; our head is in heaven. We are pilgrims in this world. We are looking for a city whose builder and maker is God, and we will occupy that city when Jesus comes and we are caught up to meet Him in the air. We will then receive our glorified bodies and our reward. The church will never be at home as long as it is in this world.

Notice that Jesus is referred to in this verse as the great God. Nowhere in the Bible do we find any teaching of the coming of God the Father. The word *appearing* is never used in the New Testament with regard to God the Father. Thus, this verse clearly teaches that Jesus is God.

So in conclusion, this grace of God which redeems also reforms and rewards. Such is the nature of the educating power of His grace.

CHAPTER THIRTY-FOUR

Submission and Superiority

Titus 3:1-3

A Christian Mindset of Submission (vv. 1-2)

Christian behavior in contemporary society was of utmost importance for the furtherance of the Gospel. No new advice, therefore, needs to be given to these Cretan Christians for Titus is to put them in mind to be subject. This verb "to be subject" shows clearly the Christian's duty towards civil administration.

The descriptive words "principalities and powers" are combined several times in Paul's writings, and they generally refer to spiritual agencies. But here the apostle evidently fears that the turbulent Cretans might too readily implicate the church in political agitation which would only bring the Gospel under suspicion. The phrase "principalities and powers", therefore, means "rulers and authorities." The Greek word *peitharcho* translated "to obey magistrates" expresses general conformity to the regulations of civil authorities.

Titus was to instruct the believers in the churches to be subject to lawful authority. Christians are to be subject to principalities and powers so long as those powers do not require them to denounce God, disobey Him, or knowingly go against His will. We are to obey the Lord in all things, and we are to be subject to magistrates and

293

rulers so long as they do not cause us to denounce God or knowingly sin against in Him in what we do or say.

The Christian should be ready to perform every good work in the community in which he lives. Where good citizenship demands communal action, he must always be cooperative, provided no question of conscience is involved.

The believer should be ready at all times to help with every good work. There are many good things in which we can participate and to which we can lend our influence, our finances, and our support, which are not directly connected with the church. There are good civic organizations which perform duties that are good and needful. We should be willing to help any cause that will help those in need, help our country or our fellow man in the things that are right and honest and decent.

This should be done without slander. To refrain from slander, to speak evil of no man, requires considerable grace, but it does much to commend the Gospel. The idea is that we are not to slander, revile, or defame anyone. We are not to say anything about another for the express purpose of doing him an injury. If it is necessary to comment about a person, even though it is the truth, we should never do this for the purpose of revenge or to find pleasure in it. In telling the truth, we should be very careful to state only what we know and not color our statements with evil insinuations.

Christians should not be brawlers, but gentle. The Christian should show all meekness meaning that he should show perfect courtesy toward all men. The

Submission and Superiority

Christian should be gentle. A brawler is a man who is contentious or easy to pick a quarrel. Paul is saying to Titus, "Put them in mind that they are not to be quarrelsome, taking offence on every issue. They are not to be always going around with a chip on the shoulder, daring someone to knock it off." Instead of being contentious, the believers in the churches were to demonstrate humility, gentleness, and meekness at all times and toward all classes of people. Whether to those in authority or to those who are poor and of very humble class, believers are to be kind without distinction.

A Christian Message of Superiority (v. 3)

As in 2:11-15, a theological statement is made to support the practical exhortations just given. If Titus should despair of the Cretan character, he should remember his own past experience, for retrospect is often beneficial in helping us to understand the magnitude of God's grace. The past is described by means of a list of vices which may at first seem exaggerated, yet Paul, elsewhere, uses similar language of his converts' pre-Christian experience.

We, who are Christians now, once conformed to this picture of wickedness. The "we" also includes Paul and Titus. The verse does not necessarily mean that every believer has been guilty of all the things pointed out here. Some things are mentioned that no doubt Paul was not guilty of before his conversion; but he is simply pointing out to Titus that he should preach to the people in the churches over which he is appointed pastor that they should live holy lives, and especially manifest a spirit of humility, order, peace, kindness, and due submission to local authorities. Titus should point out to the believers that they were formerly disorderly, wicked, and sensual; they were sinners by nature. Having heard the Gospel, through the power of that Gospel they had been saved from these things by the grace of God. Now they were new creations in Christ Jesus, and by their daily practices should prove to unbelievers that they have had a change of heart.

The minister should remember that before his conversion he was in the same condition as the unbeliever to whom he now preaches. The minister is to exhort the wicked to repent. Remembering his own life of sin and wickedness will help him fervently preach the grace of God which worked a miracle in his own heart. Having had a miracle of grace performed in his own heart, he knows what the grace of God can do for all who will receive it.

Titus was to demonstrate humility in his preaching, remembering that before his conversion, he, too, was foolish. This word is sometimes a term of reproach, denoting ungodliness and wickedness; here, however, it denotes weakness or dullness. When the apostle says that we ourselves also were sometimes foolish, he means that we were without spiritual understanding.

In Luke 24:25, Jesus rebukes the disciples for not seeing what had been prophesied by the prophets and what He himself had so clearly taught them during His public ministry. In so doing, Christ calls His disciples

Submission and Superiority

"fools." The word signifies senseless, unworthy lack of understanding. It sometimes carries with it a moral reproach and describes one who does not govern his lusts. Paul is saying to Titus, "You and I were sometimes foolish. We were thoughtless; dull, as having to do with our spiritual life and the eternity that faces us."

It is foolish for any person to go on serving the devil and sin, knowing that from the standpoint of common sense, man did not just happen upon this earth, and surely the God who created man must and will mete out justice to every man. All sinners are foolish to serve sin. If you are not a born-again child of God, you are following a foolish route; you are living a foolish life.

Next in the list is disobedience. The word signifies an unwillingness to be persuaded, spurning belief, obstinate rejection of the will of God. Unbelievers are disobedient to the law, to their parents, to civil authority, and most of all they are disobedient to God. The whole duty of man is to fear God and keep His commandments (Ecclesiastes 12:13).

It is natural for man to be disobedient; parents well know this. We do not need to teach our children to be disobedient, because disobedience is born in the hearts of all who come into this world. It is natural for the natural man to disobey God, parents, civil authority, the laws of nature, and everything else with which he comes in contact. Until the natural man is born again and becomes a new man with a new heart and a new spirit, he will be disobedient.

Now if the sin of disobedience is primarily directed

toward God, the sin of deception is primarily directed toward man. The Greek word for "deceived" suggests a false guide leading astray. We were led astray into error, seduced to wander, to be out of the way, deceiving one's self. All unbelievers are deceived. The devil is the master deceiver. A definite characteristic of the natural man is that he sees nothing in its true light; he walks amidst constant, changing illusions. He is deceived, but when the natural man becomes a born-again believer, he sees through the eyes of the Spirit.

Next, the metaphor of slavery is used to illustrate the Christian's former servitude to lusts and pleasures. That is, "Titus, before we were born again, you and I were guilty of indulging in passions, lusts, pleasures; but now we have a new heart with new desires. Before we were converted we were under the influence of different kinds of lusts and pleasures. We obeyed the call of lust. But now, the Holy Spirit leads us." Only the freed man can appreciate to the full the abjectness of his former state of slavery.

Living, or spending time in malice and envy, reflects the essentially anti-social nature of the former life. Both words emphasize malignity. The Greek word here translated "malice" means vicious character. Envy means that unbelievers live in displeasure at the happiness and prosperity of their fellow man. Unbelievers have hearts filled with covetousness, desiring what others have, never satisfied with what they themselves have; therefore, they do not have peace of mind or happiness. They live in envy, seeing what their fellow men have, and lamenting the fact that they do not have it.

Submission and Superiority 299

The climax is reached in "hateful and hating." The Greek word here translated "hateful" does not occur anywhere else in the New Testament. It means "odious" and signifies the conduct of the unbeliever is such as to be worthy of the hatred of others. Most of us who are born again will admit that before our conversion we were hateful in many ways and very unlovable. No one but God Almighty could love human beings. I am glad that God loved me while I was so unlovely; were it not for the love of God I would be lost.

When you couple this with the fact that we were hating one another, you see the state of degradation. We were hopeless. There is little brotherly love among unbelievers. The unbeliever loves himself. Generally, one who does not know God lives for self and for this world, laying up treasures on earth, satisfying the lust of his own heart, caring little for others. Paul is instructing Titus to remember all this, and declares that this is reason enough why Christians should not allow themselves to be proud and haughty, but should be gentle even toward those who are evil, knowing that they are deceived and blinded, in bondage.

We have the Gospel that will liberate unbelievers and set them free. We who know Jesus have the truth, and we can preach that truth to unbelievers, thereby helping them to see the folly and foolishness of serving the devil. We who are born again have nothing to brag about or boast about except the grace of God that saves us. This is what makes the message of Christianity superior.

CHAPTER THIRTY-FIVE

A Concentration on Salvation

Titus 3:4-7

The Basis of Salvation (vv. 4-5a)

In verse three, Paul painted a dark backdrop of our pre-Christian days. Against this dark background shines God's love in the Gospel. In verse three, Paul describes the natural man (himself and Titus included) before the love of God came into their hearts. Now God's love in the Gospel is described in verse four in a two-fold way.

The first word, *kindness*, is exclusively Pauline. Paul often uses it to describe God's kindness toward man. The act of redemption was one of great kindness, great goodness. And no one but God Almighty could have thought or wrought redemption. The plan of salvation as laid down in the New Testament (the only plan whereby man can be redeemed from iniquity) was born in the heart of God, and God is love.

So, Paul not only says that the kindness of God toward man appeared, but he also says that the love of God toward man appeared. This second term is the Greek word *philanthropia* meaning "love toward man." The word was commonly used of love towards individuals in distress, but when predicated of God, it denotes love to mankind at large, because from God's point of view all mankind is in a distressed state. Many times the word was used in connection with ransoming captives, and that may be the idea here.

The plan of salvation was founded on love, by God to man, and was the highest expression of God's love. Jesus on the cross was a display of God's best for man's worst.

When the kindness of God our Saviour to man was manifested, He saved us from those sins of which we had before been guilty (v. 3). The fact of the matter is that we all were sinners (Isaiah 53:6). Since we all are sinners, we all needed a Saviour, and God is that Saviour.

You will notice down in verse six that Paul calls Jesus Christ our Saviour. Thus, Paul clearly regarded Jesus Christ as God. We see here that Paul regarded salvation as a strictly Christian experience. Salvation is not through the God of man's choosing, but rather through the God of the Bible, the Lord Jesus Christ.

Paul was very careful to make known the eternal fact that man cannot become righteous by works. The plan of salvation is not based on what man can do, nor upon man's ability to live righteously (Isaiah 64:6).

If man could have saved himself by his own good works, there would have been no need of salvation through the Lord Jesus Christ. If our own good works were the basis for eternal life, the work of Christ would be unnecessary and vain. If man by his own good works or ability could save himself, then the greatest tragedy of all eternity would be the cross of the Lord Jesus Christ. But the cross was not a tragedy; it was a divine imperative (John 3:14). A "must" with God is a must.

Salvation has its origin in mercy, and because of

A Concentration on Salvation

God's great mercy we are saved. It is not by justice, for if we had our just rewards we would all be damned. Salvation was born in the heart of God, displayed in the body of Christ on the cross, and becomes ours by receiving the finished work of the Lord Jesus Christ. When we come to receive salvation, no other element enters but mercy. God does the saving; man cannot save himself, nor can he help God save him. We are saved entirely apart from our own efforts. We simply exercise faith in the finished work of Jesus Christ, and for Christ's sake, according to God's mercy, He saves us.

The negative statement, "not by works of righteousness which we have done", is intended to bring out by way of contrast the absolute character of the divine mercy in the next phrase. The word *righteousness* here denotes observance of the Mosaic law. The apostle was deeply conscious of the impossibility of attaining salvation by means of human effort. It is God Himself who has brought it about according to His mercy. This is a theme of which the apostle never tired.

The Means of Salvation (v. 5b)

We are saved by the washing of regeneration. The washing of regeneration refers to the hearing of the Word of God (cf. John 15:3). The Word of God is the living water that washes, regenerates (Ephesians 5:25-26). So the incorruptible, engrafted Word is able to save us.

The term *regeneration* was current in Stoicism for periodic restorations of the natural world. The word is sometimes used this way in the New Testament. In Matthew 19:28, for example, the word is used eschatologically of the new birth of the entire creation. Here in Titus 3:5 the word takes on a new meaning in view of the Christian new birth which is applied not cosmically but personally. Every believer is a new creation (II Corinthians 5:17). Each believer is conceived as a possessor of powers previously unknown.

Thus the term *renewing* specifies the renovation which accompanies regeneration. The one points to the act of entering, while the other marks the quality of the new life. Sometimes we use the word *renewal* to suggest the restoration of former powers but the term actually means "to make new." Through the work of the Holy Spirit, the believer lives on a plane that he could never achieve apart from the Spirit of God.

The Holy Spirit is the author of the new birth. Thus, we have two spiritual parents: the Word of God and the Spirit of God. These two conceive a new creation, a new man who has different desires than those of unregenerate man.

The Results of Salvation (vv. 6-7)

Greek authorities tell us that the phrase "which He shed on us" literally reads "which He poured out upon us." This same word is used of God pouring out the Spirit on the day of Pentecost (Acts 2:17). Some commentators believe that Paul, because he uses an aorist tense verb in Titus 3:6, is looking back to this historic occasion when the Spirit was poured out at Pentecost.

While there may be a remote inference to Pentecost,

A Concentration on Salvation

clearly here Paul has a direct regard for something that he and Titus experienced personally. Paul says the Holy Ghost was shed on us abundantly. Just as the Spirit was poured out abundantly on the day of Pentecost, so every believer at the very moment of conversion receives a pouring out of God's Spirit. We could say that at the time of salvation, each person experiences a Pentecost in the sense that God's Spirit is decisively and totally poured out on that individual.

The sense is that the Holy Spirit has been imparted richly to all who were converted, at any time or place. What the Apostle says here is true of all who become Christians in any age or land. We cannot do anything to merit the Holy Spirit. The Holy Spirit is poured out abundantly, richly, by the Lord Almighty when we become saved (Romans 8:9). One receives the Holy Spirit when he is saved, and if one does not have the Spirit, he does not belong to Christ.

The Greek word translated here "abundantly" is translated elsewhere in the New Testament "richly." It is used in Colossians 3:16 of the Word dwelling in us richly. It is used in I Timothy 6:17 of God giving to us richly. Paul uses it here to show us that God does not give the Holy Spirit niggardly. When one is saved, Jesus richly, extravagantly, pours out His Spirit upon that person.

The believer also receives a new standing. There is no denying the characteristic Pauline flavor of these next words: being justified by His grace. Paul again points out that salvation is not by works; works have never saved anyone, and they never will. The grace of

God makes us just. Grace becomes ours through faith. When we exercise faith in the finished work of Jesus, God's grace becomes ours and we are justified in the sight of God.

When God the Father looks at believers, He sees the blood, and in His sight we are just as pure as the blood that covers us. Since we are justified by God's grace, we are sons of God. God has received us as His children. We belong to the family of God, and He has made us heirs.

In the New Testament, justification and righteousness are inseparable. The Greek word *dikaios* is translated "righteous", and the Greek word *dikaioo* is translated "to justify." The believing sinner is justified because Christ, having borne his sins on the cross, has been made unto him righteousness. Justification which has its beginning in grace is through the redemptive work of Christ.

Justification is the judicial act of God, whereby God simply declares righteous those who believe on Jesus Christ as Saviour. The justified person, relying entirely on the finished work of Christ, has been in court, God's court, only to learn that nothing is laid to his charge. Jesus, through His redemptive work, paid the sin-debt in full, and when the unbeliever trusts in the Lord Jesus as Saviour, the blood covers all sin making the guilty one justified. He has a new standing.

Now the phrase "being justified" is an amplification of the previous phrase "he saved us" and the latter part of verse seven tells us why He saved us. He saved us in

A Concentration on Salvation

order that we should be made heirs. The point of reference to justification at this point is that no one who is not justified can hope for an inheritance. Paul brought out this same idea in Galatians 3, where he begins verse eleven by talking about justification and ends the section in verse 29 talking about us being heirs according to the promise. There is no inheritance apart from justification.

An heir is one who succeeds to another's property upon the other's death. We who are heirs of God shall be partakers of that inheritance which God confers upon those who accept Jesus Christ as Saviour. That inheritance is eternal life here and hereafter. Romans 8:17 tells us that we are joint heirs with Christ. Christians are united to Christ, and they are thus positionally destined to partake with Him of His glory and all the glories of heaven.

This connection between Christ and Christians is often referred to in the New Testament. The fact that we are united to Christ is often given as an assurance that we will be united hereafter (John 14:19). Our position to Christ guarantees our future (II Timothy 2:11-12).

As heirs, we are not yet possessors in the fullest sense. The phrase "according to the hope" clearly shows this. Nevertheless, the term *hope* in the Bible always conveys solid assurance because Bible hope is rooted and based on the promises of God (cf. 1:2). On the basis of this hope, the justified believer may look forward towards the full appropriation of his inheritance.

The words do not exclude any present possession of

life, but rather anticipate its complete realization. Thus, we not only have a new Spirit, and a new standing, but also a new sonship which will reach its ultimate realization in heaven.

CHAPTER THIRTY-SIX

True and False Teaching

Titus 3:8-11

True Teaching (v. 8)

The phrase "faithful saying" relates to the previous statement (vv. 4-7), which may be regarded as an epitome of Pauline theology. The reference here is to the doctrine just stated as to how we are saved and justified, the doctrine of salvation by grace through faith in the finished work of Jesus. This is of great importance in the word of God. There is no doctrine more important than that of salvation by grace. Therefore, this is a faithful saying, and these things should be constantly preached without apology. The primary message of the Bible is salvation. Reaching unbelievers and saving sinners is the nearest, dearest thing to the heart of God.

The keynote of this epistle has been that God has not only saved us from a penalty of sin, but that God has also saved us from the power of sin. Thus, once salvation has been embraced, the message of grace tells us that those who have believed in God should be careful to maintain good works. Thus, the phrase "these things" may look back to all the injunctions which Paul has told Timothy to preach.

This sets forth Paul's belief that the doctrines of the Gospel would lead men to holy living. "Good works" here refers not only to acts of benevolence and charity, but also has to do with all that is holy. The verb here translated "affirm constantly" is the Greek word *diabebaioomai*, a word Paul used of the false teachers with whom Timothy had to deal (I Timothy 1:7). These teachers were affirming things they didn't understand. Titus, on the other hand, as well as all ministers of the Gospel, should affirm things because they do understand them.

These affirmations toward holy living are to be particularly directed to those which have believed in God. There are two corollaries we can derive from this. The first is that it is impossible to teach an unbeliever the things of God. One must be born again before he can understand Christian conduct (I Corinthians 2:14). The second corollary is that a true belief is an indispensable basis for the right ordering of conduct.

So, the Christian minister has a specific charge to encourage believers to have a thoughtful approach to the maintenance of good works. They are to be teaching their parishioners to be careful to maintain good works.

The grace of God should always be the subject of the pastor's teaching. There should be no occasion when God's minister does not incorporate into his message the plan of salvation according to the Scriptures and the product of salvation which is the maintenance of good works.

The Bible doctrines here stated are not mere matters of speculation. They are ordained of God and were given to promote human happiness and spiritual prosperity. These doctrines should be consistently preached

True and False Teaching   311

and taught in all churches by God's ministers.

False Teaching (vv. 9-11)

Just as there were some things that Titus was to engage in, so there were some things that Titus was to avoid. The word *periistemi* literally means "to turn oneself about so as to face the other way." The basic reason given for such avoidance is the essential unprofitableness and uselessness of the false teaching. This consideration might well be borne in mind by all who undertake the pastoral office. Avoid false teaching.

You may have heard some people say that no question is dumb. Well, this is not a Bible position. The Bible says, "Avoid foolish questions." There is a stupidity prevalent among these so-called teachers, and the thing that revealed their stupidity was their questions; they were foolish.

Their teaching was characterized by genealogies. Paul told Timothy to watch out for genealogies (1 Timothy 1:4), and earlier in this epistle when Paul had told Titus to watch out for false teachers, he reminded his pastor friend that this false system was Jewish in nature (1:10). Here again in chapter three, Paul brings out the Jewish character again by mentioning "genealogies."

This clearly refers to Jewish teachings. The Hebrews kept careful records, so that in the course of time they might, without much exaggeration, be called "endless." The Jews attached great importance to these records and were very careful to preserve them.

In John 8, the Jews were very angry with Jesus, and

in the course of their conversation they proudly threw in His face the assertion that they were of Abraham's seed and did not need to be set free from sin.

Now the Saviour has come, and the middle wall has been broken down between Jews and Gentiles (Ephesians 2:13-14). The distinction of tribes is now useless, and there is no reason for these endless genealogies to be regarded by Christians. The whole Jewish system served to keep up great pride of blood and birth, which was definitely opposed to Christianity.

Two words are used here to show why these questions and genealogies are so wrong. They were wrong because they fostered "contentions" and "strivings." The subject matter over which these quarrels arose, is the law, which must refer to the Mosaic law.

Titus was to warn the people not only against foolish questions, genealogies, and contentions, but also against strivings about the law. The Jews took great joy and pride in advertising their knowledge and authority on the law of Moses. They followed Jesus continually with the one desire to trap Him, asking Him questions concerning the Sabbath, washing of hands, tithing, and various subjects having to do with the law. Jesus assured them that He had not come to destroy the law, but to fulfill it — every jot and tittle. The Jews loved to discuss the law as having to do with meats, drinks, holy days, and holidays. But we are reminded that Christianity is not meats and drinks, and days, but Christ in you, the hope of glory. Christianity is a person, not a system.

Paul declares that such strivings and discussions

True and False Teaching   313

are unprofitable and vain. I am sure that most of God's ministers (myself included) have wasted precious time in talking about frivolities and arguing points of doctrine, when we should have been lifting up the Lord Jesus Christ. Any person, if he is saved and surrendered to the Lord God Almighty, will automatically fall into line with Bible doctrine. A spiritually-minded person will read the Bible and accept the Word of God, refusing traditions and doctrines of men.

To argue and strive about foolish questions only leads to hard feelings. Oftentimes, these discussions are very difficult to settle and lead into serious spiritual conditions in the local assembly. There is much disputing today, pro and con, but little time is spent obeying the Great Commission.

The Greek word translated "heretic" does not appear as it is used here elsewhere in the New Testament. The true meaning of the word as used here is "one who promotes a party or a sect religiously." Simpson has defined a heretic as "an opinionative propagandist who promotes dissension by his pertinacity." This idea is brought out for us in Romans 16:17. The term might be applied to those who make divisions in the local church, instead of striving to promote unity and peace. Such a person may form his own sect or group, teaching what he chooses on some point of doctrine, independently of the church. Thus, in disagreement, he sets up his own little sect or religion. According to the Scriptures, such a man is a heretic.

In later times, the word acquired a more technical

meaning of one who holds false doctrine. The word *heretic* today is applied to anyone who holds some fundamental error of doctrine. Webster defines a heretic as "one who holds and teaches opinions repugnant to the established faith, or that which is made the standard of orthodoxy."

The first approach to these false teachers is to be by means of admonition. The word here is *nouthesia*, Paul's technical term for warning. The lenience advocated is striking, for it is only on the third occasion of admonition that the more serious action of avoidance is to be taken.

The pastor and the people are not to be hasty or rash in dealing with the heretic. Give him an opportunity to explain himself and state his reason for acting as he does. Give him an opportunity to repent and abandon his heresy. All men under all circumstances should be given an opportunity to repent, and, then, after the first and second admonition, if the heretic refuses to repent, he is to be turned out of the church.

A different word is used here to denote avoidance than that used in verse nine. The word translated "reject" is the Greek term *paraiteomai*, a vague term which means "to leave out of account." The word is translated "refuse" in Acts 25:11 and "avoid" in II Timothy 2:23. Thus, such a person should not be admitted into the membership in the church. If such a person does not repent after two admonitions, he is to be excused from the body.

If this action seems harsh, Titus has to remember

True and False Teaching

that this man's stubbornness is evidence of a perverted mind. The sinning mentioned here has to be understood in light of the previous verses, the desire to promote dissension. It is useless to contend with men of twisted minds, and there is no need to condemn them, for they are self-condemned.

The man who is a heretic has turned from the right way; he has turned from the truth of the faith once delivered to the saints. Literally, he is turned out. Such a one should be rejected, and believers should withdraw fellowship from him.

This verse does not necessarily teach that the heretic will have a self-accusing conscience. In many instances the conscience of a heretic is seared. The reference, therefore, seems not to be so much a deliberate act of condemning oneself, but to the fact that perverted and sinful action in the end automatically condemns the doer.

CHAPTER THIRTY-SEVEN

Concluding Remarks

Titus 3:12-15

To the Pastor (vv. 12-13)

Concerning Artemas and Tychicus (v. 12)

Artemas is not mentioned anywhere else in the New Testament. We know nothing about him, but undoubtedly he was a true believer, possibly converted under Paul's ministry.

Tychicus is mentioned in Acts 20:4, Ephesians 6:21, Colossians 4:7, and II Timothy 4:12. This man was certainly a believer and stood high in the confidence and affection of the Apostle Paul. In Ephesians 6, Paul described him as "a beloved brother and faithful minister in the Lord." In II Timothy 4, Paul sent him to Ephesus to relieve Timothy. Evidently Artemas or Tychicus was to replace Titus in Crete during the latter's absence.

It is not certain which city of Nicopolis is meant, but it is generally assumed it was the city of that name in Epirus. Although no other evidence that Paul went to Epirus exists, both here and in II Timothy 4:21, there is a reference to Paul's plan for the winter and in each case he urges his close associates to be diligent to come.

Paul is reminding Titus to be alert and make sure that he arrives in Nicopolis by winter. Just why Paul wanted to make sure Titus would visit him there, we do not know. There is no record that Paul organized a church there. We are sure that he preached the Gospel, and most assuredly there were converts; however, it could be that to Paul the field seemed to be extremely promising and this is the reason he requested Titus to leave his important post of duty on the island of Crete and come to visit him at Nicopolis.

Concerning Zenas and Apollos (v. 13)

Zenas, the lawyer, is unknown apart from this reference, but we meet with Apollos in several situations (both in Acts and I Corinthians). The word *lawyer* translates the Greek word nomikos and was used of an expert in either Hebrew or Roman law. Many people have felt that since *Zenas* is a Greek name, Roman law is in view here. The Gospels, however, would support the idea of Jewish law being the topic. This theory is buttressed by Zenas's association with Apollos, who was also familiar with Jewish law.

Zenas, the lawyer, no doubt belonged to the class of persons often referred to in the New Testament as lawyers, who dealt primarily with expounding Jewish law. It does not necessarily mean that they practiced law as we know lawyers today. It could be that there were many Jews in Nicopolis, and Paul felt that this converted lawyer might be able to win some of the Jews to Christianity by coming to visit him.

Apollos is mentioned in Acts 18:24, Acts 19:1, and in several places in I Corinthians. He was also well-skilled in the law of Moses and in Jewish law, and was

Concluding Remarks

mighty in the Scriptures (Acts 18:24). Evidently, Zenas and Apollos traveled together, perhaps already having been on a journey, probably preaching the Gospel. Paul knew of their ministry, and supposing that they would be in Crete, he therefore instructed Titus to bring them with him.

Titus is to bring these two on their journey, and the word *propempo* means "to speed them on their way." The Greek word means "speedily", that is, "Hurry up their journey, lose no time in getting started, come as quickly as possible."

There is no necessity to suppose that Zenas and Apollos were both in Crete, although that would be the most natural assumption. Titus might be expected to meet them on his way to Nicopolis, but since he is to see that nothing be wanting unto them (which suggests he was in a position to provide material assistance), it is better to assume that Zenas and Apollos are paying a visit to Crete and that the apostle is anxious to secure adequate hospitality for them.

These words mean that everything necessary for the journey should be supplied by the believers in Crete. Paul wanted these brethren to have hospitable treatment that would afford them the necessities of life to make the trip comfortable. The laborer is worthy of his hire, and they that preach the Gospel shall live of the Gospel. Paul did not want these ministers embarrassed by the want of that which was needful for their journey and which would make them comfortable in their travels.

To the People (vv. 14-15)

Concerning finances (v. 14)

After these specific instructions to Titus, a general exhortation is added directed to "ours", that is, our people. Clearly the Cretan Christians are intended, for these people are to learn to maintain good works. The people must really learn to make themselves practically useful.

The practical side of Christianity is here brought into vivid focus. The words "for necessary uses" should probably be understood as a reference to cases of urgent need. All who engage in such works of mercy need never fear that they will be unfruitful.

Paul had just instructed Titus to aid Zenas and Apollos, and here he adds that he desires the same as pertaining to all the believers in Crete. That is, all the believers should give to these travelling ministers, that their needs might be met.

All believers should be distinguished for good works — including benevolent deeds, acts of charity, honest labor, and whatever would enter into the conception of an upright life. We should be diligent to work, and by so doing, glorify God and help our brothers and sisters who are believers.

Our duty to our families and our duty to other families who may be in need necessitates this. Even friends and strangers should be assisted with food and shelter when necessary. Believers should be charitable and dili-

Concluding Remarks

gent in good works. In so doing, all may see that our religion is not barren, but produces a fruitful life—a life of charity toward not only the church, but society as a whole (cf. Ephesians 4:28). We prove to the world that our Christianity is genuine by what we do, not by what we say. We can talk long and loud, but if our actions do not back up what we say, then the world will watch what we do and will not listen to what we say. I had rather see a sermon than hear one, any day.

Concerning farewells (v. 15)

In most of Paul's epistles, he closes by naming those who send love and salutation, but in this closing it is implied that Titus himself had been travelling with Paul and that he knew those who were with him. Paul evidently refers not to those who were residing in the place where he was, but to those who had gone with him from Crete as his believing companions and fellow-helpers. There is no means of identifying all who were with Paul. This linking of fellow workers with him in the conclusion is thoroughly characteristic.

The description "them that love us in the faith" brings a most intimate touch into the otherwise rather vague greetings. The absence of the article before "faith" may mean that we are not meant to take this as a reference to the Christian faith. Oliver B. Greene believes the reference here is to the faith of the gospel, the faith once delivered to the saints. Easton, similarly, translates it "those who love us as Christians." The absence of the definite article in Greek may be meant to symbolize "those who love us faithfully."

The final benediction is identical with those of I and II Timothy, except for the insertion of the word *all*. Paul begins his letters to the churches in grace, and he closes in grace. He was extremely jealous for preaching the grace of God. The Apostle Paul was converted on the road to Damascus (Acts 9). From that day until his head fell into Nero's basket, grace was his primary topic.

The book of Titus is no exception. Paul preached the grace of God which redeems, which reforms, and which rewards. The book begins and ends with grace.